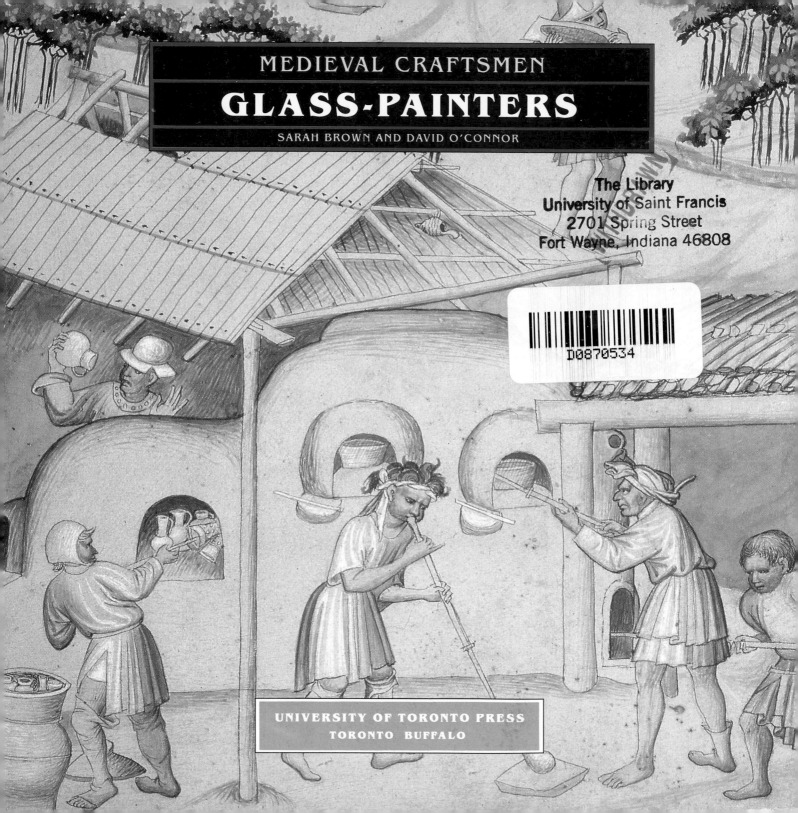

MEDIEVAL CRAFTSMEN

GLASS-PAINTERS

SARAH BROWN AND DAVID O'CONNOR

UNIVERSITY OF TORONTO PRESS
TORONTO BUFFALO

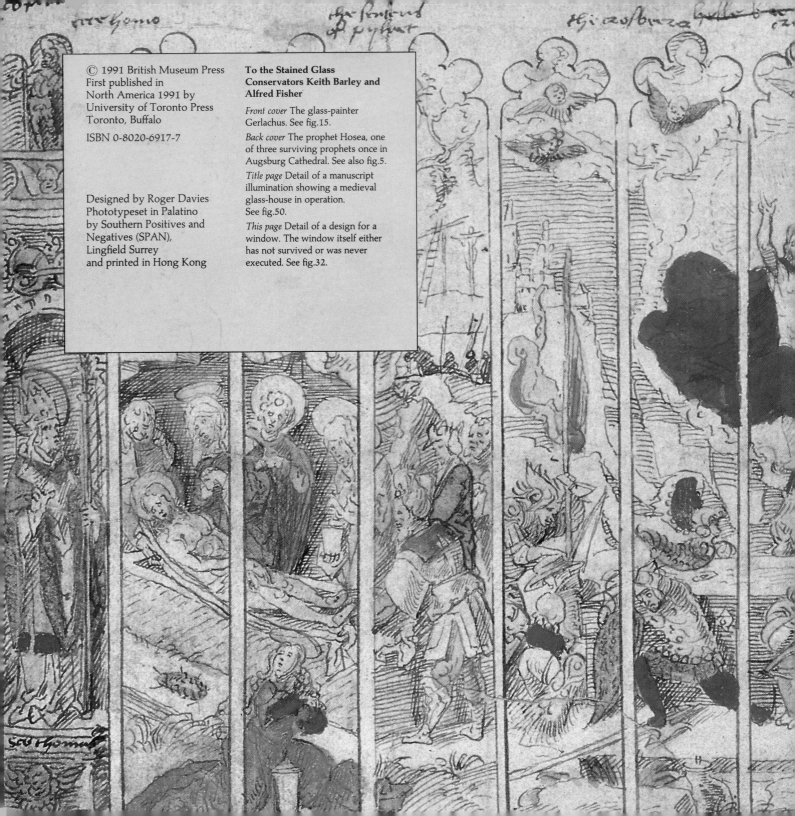

© 1991 British Museum Press
First published in
North America 1991 by
University of Toronto Press
Toronto, Buffalo

ISBN 0-8020-6917-7

Designed by Roger Davies
Phototypeset in Palatino
by Southern Positives and
Negatives (SPAN),
Lingfield Surrey
and printed in Hong Kong

**To the Stained Glass
Conservators Keith Barley and
Alfred Fisher**

Front cover The glass-painter
Gerlachus. See fig.15.

Back cover The prophet Hosea, one
of three surviving prophets once in
Augsburg Cathedral. See also fig.5.

Title page Detail of a manuscript
illumination showing a medieval
glass-house in operation.
See fig.50.

This page Detail of a design for a
window. The window itself either
has not survived or was never
executed. See fig.32.

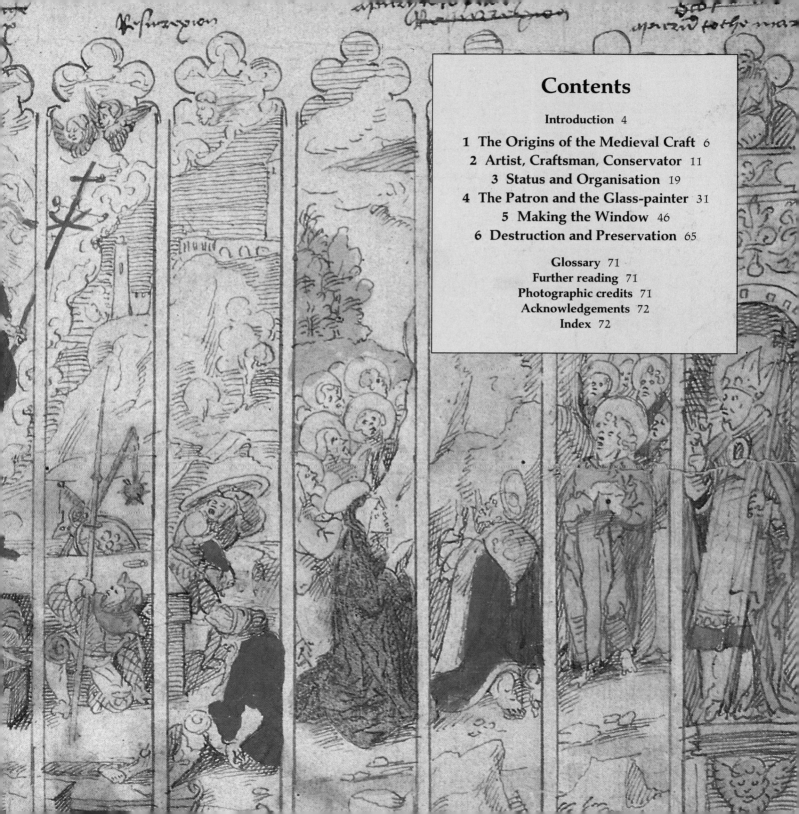

Contents

INTRODUCTION

Most medieval artists and craftsmen remain anonymous, but the resulting obscurity has been particularly impenetrable as far as glass-painters are concerned. Very little has been written on the lives and careers of those who were responsible for one of the most public of all medieval arts. The names of outstanding glass-painters – John Thornton, Peter Hemmel or Engrand Le Prince, for example – are not widely known, whereas manuscript illuminators like Jean Pucelle or the Limbourg Brothers, panel painters like Jan van Eyck, and sculptors such as Claus Sluter, have all been the subjects of major art historical studies. Had the finest glass-painters worked instead on canvas or panel their reputation would no doubt be similarly established. It is profoundly ironic that outstanding glass-painters, working in a medium which after all is concerned with light, should end up in relative obscurity.

The reasons for this are that documentary evidence for their activities is often scarce; it frequently relates to lost works and its interpretation may be problematic in other ways. In addition, medieval stained glass contains the seeds of its own destruction for the glass of that period is subject to chemical deterioration and the lead which holds the windows together has a limited life. Furthermore, stained glass has been the object of deliberate programmes of destruction at the hands of iconoclasts from the sixteenth century onwards; general neglect, war and changes in fashion have taken their toll on this most vulnerable of art forms. An appreciation of the glass-painter's craft all too often requires a considerable feat of creative imagination from the onlooker eager to reconstruct the original appearance and effect of the window, when the images themselves may often be scarcely legible. A visitor to a huge cathedral such as Chartres, Cologne or York Minster can be forgiven for finding the overall effect of the windows impressive but the meaning of the individual panels baffling.

Interest in the medium may also have suffered from a widespread lack of understanding of the techniques of the glass-painter's craft. The situation is further clouded for the layman by potentially confusing terminology: in the English language the term 'stained glass' is used in a very wide sense for what might, more accurately, be referred to as 'painted glass'. The term is derived from one specific glass-painting technique, yellow stain, a method of colouring white glass yellow. This was not invented until the early years of the fourteenth century, but nevertheless, 'stained glass' is the term used for leaded windows made before and after its invention, and whether or not the windows are coloured or grisaille (predominantly white glass). Brown or black paint, employed in the Middle Ages for drawing and shading, was used for windows, although not all were painted. Sometimes the yellow stain technique was employed, but again, not always. Only in the post-medieval period was the palette of 'paintable' colours enlarged with the development of enamel glass-painting which was alien to the traditional medieval craft in nearly every respect. The English artist-craftsman Christopher Whall even refused to admit this type of glass-painting into his definition of stained glass, writing in his technical manual of 1905 that: 'stained glass means pieces of coloured glass put together with strips of lead into the forms of windows; not a picture painted on glass with coloured paints'.

In languages other than English this confusion between painting and staining is less acute. In German, the medium is called *die Glasmalerei* and in French *le vitrail*. In fact, in all three languages, the term for the artist – *Glasmaler, peintre-verrier* and glass-painter – are almost equal in according the painter of glass the same linguistic status as artists working on vellum, in fresco, or on panel.

Because of a combination of historical circumstances, glass-painters, unlike artists working in many other media, were not able to sustain the tradition of their art beyond the end of the Middle Ages. This break in tradition saw the reputation of the medium decline and its practitioners relegated in time to the status of craftsmen. Many of the illustrations in this book, showing the work of some of the outstanding glass-painters of the Middle Ages, serve to confirm at a glance the view of the Victorian historian of stained glass, Charles Winston, who stated firmly that 'glass-painting was once practised by artists'.

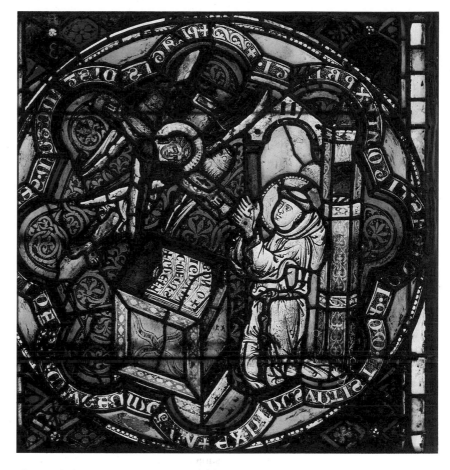

This panel of 1230–5 depicts an event that took place in 1224, the stigmatisation of St Francis. The wounds in his hands and side, which are visible in this panel, together with those in his feet, remained hidden until his death in 1226. He was canonised in 1228, but his order was already widespread throughout Europe. The Franciscan Barfüsserkirche in Erfurt contains one of the earliest and most important cycles of Franciscan iconography to survive anywhere in Europe.

1 THE ORIGINS OF THE MEDIEVAL CRAFT

The medieval glass-painter inherited a long tradition of craftsmanship in glass. This chapter outlines the earliest development of the medium. Glass has been used for many thousands of years. In prehistoric times man fashioned obsidian, a natural glass formed by the intense heat of volcanoes, into tools and weapons. A glassy paste known as faience was widely used in the ancient world for the manufacture of beads and figurines. When and where man-made glass originated is not known, although more than three thousand years before the birth of Christ, somewhere in the eastern Mediterranean, this translucent, light and decorative material was first created and endowed with magical associations. Writing in the third century AD, Pliny the Elder, in his *Historia Naturalis*, maintained that it was Phoenician sailors who accidently discovered it in the embers of their camp fire on the shore of the River Belus. Such a chance discovery seems plausible, although it is thought that it was Syrian craftsmen who first perfected the manufacture of glass.

The Egyptians quickly recognised its potential and used it for simple moulded and pressed vessels, beads, decorative inlays and even figurines. In 1370 BC the Pharaoh Thothmes established a glass vessel industry at Tel-el-Amarna, and nineteenth-century excavations on the site uncovered a remarkable range of coloured glasses, including black, two shades of blue, a bright violet, two greens, a yellow and rich red. Egyptian glass vessels were luxury items, such as ointment pots, unguent bottles, statuettes of deities and vessels for grave goods. The invention of the blowpipe in about 40 BC, probably in Syria or Israel, changed this for ever. Mouth-blown vessels could be mass produced cheaply and in more complex and varied shapes and it was this technology which was later exploited in medieval glass-houses to produce the raw materials for the glass-painter.

The Roman taste for both decorative and functional glass stimulated the profitable expansion of the glass industry in the Middle East and glass-makers soon settled in Rome itself. They were so numerous by the third century AD that they occupied a specific quarter of the city and a tax was levied on them. Indeed, it was the Romans who first appreciated the enormous and varied potential of this material, which produced such masterpieces as the first-century Portland Vase and the fifth-century Lycurgus Cup (both in the British Museum). The domestic use of glass was more common in the Roman Empire than in any other era before the nineteenth century.

The use of glass in an architectural context was relatively slow to develop. The Romans used it in windows, although it was but one of a number of more or less translucent materials, including mica, alabaster and shell, that were set into decorative frames of wood, plaster or bronze. The pieces of glass employed were

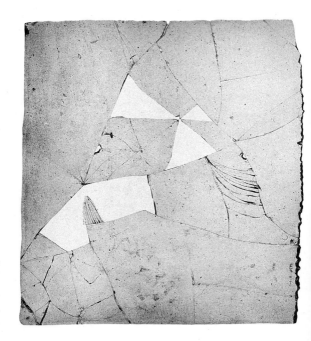

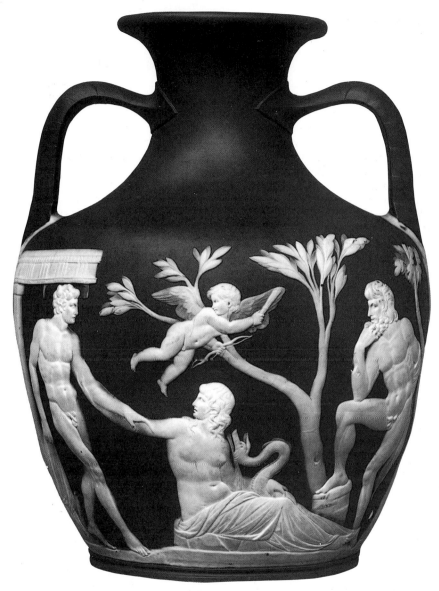

small and were cast rather than blown. By the fall of the Empire there were well-established glass industries throughout the Roman world and window glass has been excavated at Hartfield in East Sussex and at Caerleon in Wales. Surviving examples sometimes bear the surface imprint of the trays of sand and wood into which the molten glass was poured and spread flat. There is plentiful literary and increasing archaeological evidence for the widespread use of such *claustra* or *transennae*, throughout the Roman and Muslim worlds. Fifth-century alabaster transennae were found in the church of San Appollinare in Classe in Ravenna and eleventh- and twelfth-century examples survive in Torcello Cathedral and San Cataldo in Palermo. The gradual replacement of the plaster or wood lattices by malleable lead created a flexible and more versatile construction. The introduction of lead into window construction cannot be dated with any precision, but it has been plausibly suggested that it was the use of metal strips to separate areas of colour in the manufacture of enamels which first suggested its use to craftsmen in glass. After the invention of the blowpipe, it was the second key technology of the medieval glass-painter.

Decorative glass windows appeared in Christian churches at a very early date. In describing Constantinople the poet Prudentius (348–c.410) was impressed by the widespread use of glass when he wrote 'In the round arches of the windows in the basilica shone glass in colours without number'. As colour rather than subject matter is stressed here, it is possible that many early glazing schemes consisted of abstract coloured mosaics rather than painted, historiated windows.

The appeal of stained glass to the Christian Church was both aesthetic and spiritual in its origin. In Genesis the first words spoken by God are *Fiat lux*, 'Let there be light', words pondered at length by St Augustine of Hippo (354–430), who stressed the special and divinely ordained nature of light; Genesis continues 'And God saw the light, that it was good'. St John's Gospel developed this theme and described Christ as *Lux Vera*, 'the True Light'. In this account, Christ himself twice declared 'I am the light of the

1 *Left* This panel of green moulded window-glass was excavated on the site of a Roman villa at Hartfield in East Sussex. The uneven texture of its surface suggests that the molten glass was poured into a mould lined with sand.

2 *Above* The first-century Portland Vase, prior to its recent reconstruction by the British Museum, expresses in the complexity of its shape and the delicacy of its ornament the sophistication and skill of Roman glass-craftsmen. The mythological figurative scenes are cut out of opaque white glass, cameo-style, to reveal the cobalt blue glass beneath.

world' and promised that those believing in him would become the children of light. In a striking image, the Cistercian monk St Bernard of Clairvaux (1090–1153) compared the harmless yet beautifying passage of sunlight through glass to the miraculous passage of the Holy Spirit through the Virgin Annunciate. Stained glass windows are never static; in the course of the day they are animated by changing light and a building illuminated by them is diffused with that very element most closely connected with God, the element which St Augustine argued most expressly received divine approval.

No complete windows survive from the fifth and sixth centuries, although literary evidence for them is plentiful. Sidonius Appollinaris in the fifth century describes the church windows of Lyons as having multicoloured figures, and in the following century, Gregory of Tours lists a number of Frankish churches with coloured glass windows. In seventh-century England the craft of glazing, which died out when the Romans left and so was lost to the Anglo-Saxons, was reintroduced through contact with the churches of Gaul. Eddius Stephanus' life of Bishop Wilfrid describes his church in York in about 670, glazed against wind, rain and the passage of birds, but allowing the light to shine within, a neat description of the practical and aesthetic roles of the new material. Bede's *Historia Abbatum* (History of the Abbots of Monkwearmouth and Jarrow) reveals that in 675 Abbot Benedict Biscop sent to Gaul for craftsmen both to make and to glaze the windows of his monastery church at Monkwearmouth in Northumbria. Excavations both here and at nearby Jarrow have uncovered coloured but unpainted fragments of window glass of this period.

An important characteristic of most stained glass is, of course, the application of paint to its coloured surface, which both released its enormous decorative, devotional and didactic possibilities and raised its creators to the status of artists as well as artisans. Archaeological evidence is pushing back the date of the earliest painted glass – fragments of crown glass bearing the painted outline of Christ in Benediction from San Vitale in Ravenna have been

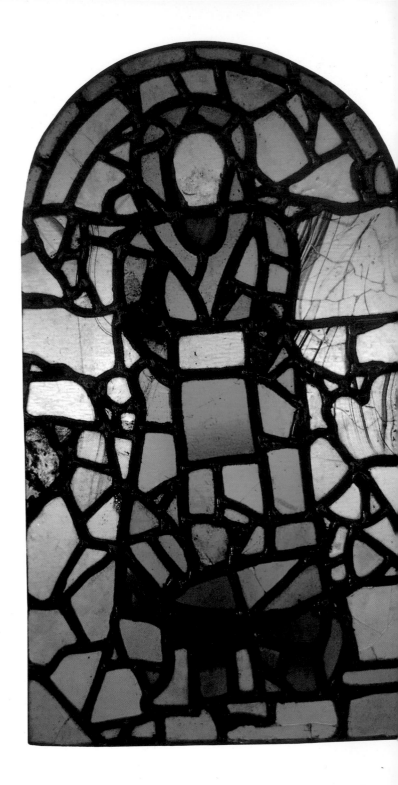

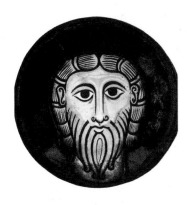

dated to as early as about 540. A leaded panel found in the cemetery of Séry-les-Mézières (Aisne), but subsequently destroyed, depicted a Greek cross with the symbols of Alpha and Omega and is believed to have dated from the ninth century. The late tenth-century chronicle of the monastery of St Rémi in Reims describes *fenestris diversas continentibus historias* (diverse windows containing stories); and the striking heads, probably of Christ, excavated from the abbeys of Lorsch in Hesse and Wissembourg in Alsace, perhaps dating to the ninth and mid eleventh centuries respectively, already bear the three-layered tonal painting described by Theophilus in the twelfth century. There are therefore adequate antecedents for the figures of prophets in the nave clerestory of Augsburg Cathedral dating to about 1100 – Jonah, Daniel and Hosea – and of Moses, a sixteenth-century copy. These four are the earliest surviving complete figures in stained glass, painted with a sophistication and assurance suggestive of an already ancient tradition.

Despite the vitality and splendour of their creations, the men, and some few women, who made medieval windows remain for the most part shadowy figures. The sources for a history of the medieval craft are scant and often ambiguous in their evidence. The documents are of an overwhelmingly financial nature; taxation records, account books and bills with only a tiny number of contracts and letters of appointment before the sixteenth century. Where a glass-painter's name survives, the window almost invariably does not, the reverse being also frustratingly common. No workshop tools survive, although in Girona in Spain the working table of a glass-painter has recently been discovered. Knowledge of their working practices is derived from a number of craftsman's manuals and from the regulations of the Guilds that ruled the profession.

Stained glass flourished as a major art form in Gothic Europe (around the mid twelfth to sixteenth centuries). It thrived in an architectural climate that sought to eliminate the solid masonry of the wall and substitute ever larger and more decorative windows. It would not be an exaggeration to regard this architectural

3 *Opposite* Fragments of unpainted coloured glass making up this figure were excavated at the Anglo-Saxon sites of Monkwearmouth and Jarrow, and retain their colour and translucency despite centuries of burial. This survival is no doubt due to their high soda content, typical of the highly durable glasses manufactured in the Roman tradition.

4 *Above* This austere eleventh-century head, probably of Christ, perfectly demonstrates the three-layered tonal style of painting described in Theophilus' treatise *De Diversis Artibus*.

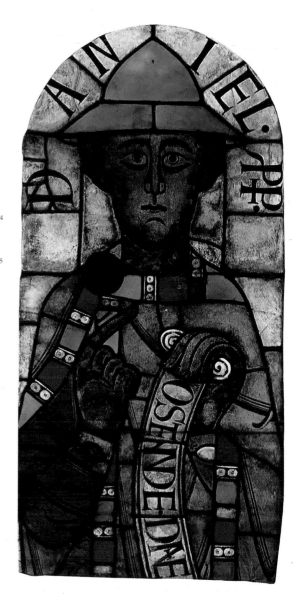

5 The prophet Daniel, here almost life-size, is one of three twelfth-century survivors (Jonah and Hosea being the other two) from an original series of twenty-two figures. Designed for clerestory windows in Augsburg Cathedral, they are not now in their original settings, but their impact is undiminished.

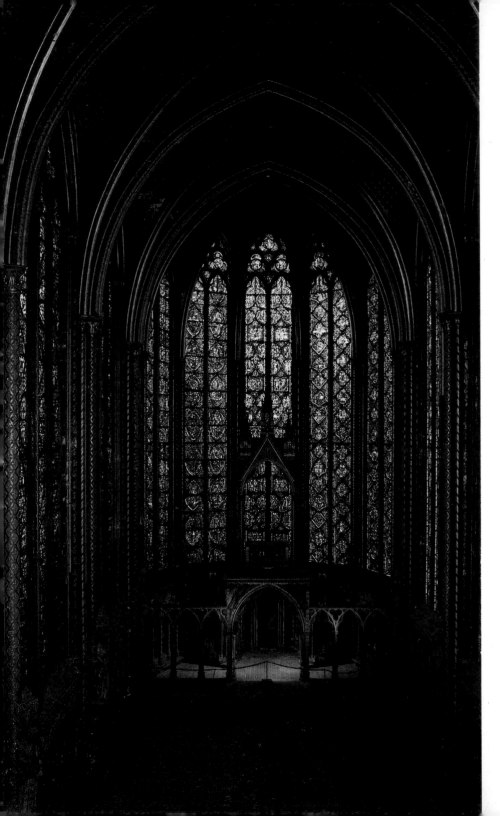

development as a reflection of the medieval 6
concept of the role of light in the ecclesiastical
interior; recording the reconstruction of the
abbey church of Saint-Denis, near Paris, in about
1140, Abbot Suger described with pride the
addition of 'a circular string of chapels, by virtue
of which the whole [church] would shine with
the wonderful and uninterrupted light of most
luminous windows, pervading the interior
beauty'. Externally the stained glass window is
often barely distinguishable from the texture of
the wall. From within it is transformed and
animated by light.

The demise of stained glass in the second half
of the sixteenth century is discussed in the final
chapter and can be attributed to a number of
factors, some of them internal — technical
innovation, changes in fashion and new materials — and some of them external — Reformation, iconoclasm, religious conflict, neglect.
However, the changing aesthetic of the period
was just as influential. The rise of classicism
fostered a distaste for the decorative vocabulary
of the Gothic stained glass window and sub-
stituted a smaller, simpler window. And yet,
despite deterioration, neglect and destruction,
many medieval windows have survived, and
their very artistic qualities prompt the search for
the glass-painters who created them.

6 Completed in 1249, the Sainte-Chapelle in Paris was
constructed by Saint Louis to house the relic of the
Crown of Thorns, purchased at colossal expense from
the Emperor of Constantinople in 1239. The relics of
the Cross and Lance were soon added to this
architectural reliquary in which the enormous stained
glass windows create the impression of a jewelled
casket.

2 ARTIST, CRAFTSMAN, CONSERVATOR

Later chapters will discuss the status of medieval glass-painters, their organisation and training, their patrons and techniques: here it is proposed to look at them in broader terms and raise a question which is still very relevant – should those who work in stained glass be regarded as artists or craftsmen?

Current conceptions, both of the medium and its practitioners, have been distorted in a number of ways. As already stated, only a fraction of the stained glass produced during the Middle Ages has survived to this day. In certain countries, Holland or Norway for example, the losses have been catastrophic; and in Britain, France and Germany, where much more has survived, windows have frequently been moved from their original settings, sold to museums or collectors, or reduced to fragments. Few medieval windows survive intact and none comes down without considerable change, for corrosion, paint loss and restoration have altered their original appearance and distorted our vision. These kinds of problems are compounded in the heavily corroded panels of fifteenth-century glass from an unknown Austrian church, which were presented to the church of Kirkby Wharfe, Yorkshire, by Lord Londesborough in 1865.

Today people have very different expectations of a work on glass by comparison with a painting on canvas, and the monetary values of the art market reinforce such prejudices. For so long, stained glass has been relegated to the position of a minor art, one of what William Morris in a telling phrase described as a 'so-called decorative art', that it is now difficult to appreciate the major role it once played in the past. When the medium itself is devalued, artists who worked in that medium not surprisingly become undervalued too.

The rise of stained glass from its obscure beginnings to a position of pre-eminence among forms of monumental painting in northern Europe has been outlined in the previous chapter. Besides playing a prominent aesthetic role by bringing light and colour into a building, stained glass windows were used as carriers of signs and images, capable of proclaiming the central truths of the Christian faith in a very direct and public way. Most mysterious of all, allying itself with prestigious jewellery and precious metalwork, the medium could be interpreted theologically as a powerful symbol of God's presence in the world.

The east window of York Minster, glazed between 1405 and 1408 under the direction of the glass-painter John Thornton of Coventry, can be used to demonstrate the contribution that stained glass artists made to the medieval cathedral. The English love of flat, cliff-like terminations to great churches allowed for huge expanses of glass, and the York window, which measures about 23.4 m by 9.8 m, acts as a vast altarpiece rising some distance behind the high altar itself, the focal point of worship in the medieval church. The masons and glaziers combined to devise a series of tracery light openings for groups of figures representing the whole company of heaven, with God at the apex holding a book inscribed: 'I am Alpha and Omega'. This theme of beginning and end extends to the main light glazing with its twenty-seven panels above the transom, representing scenes from the Creation to the Death of Absalom, all from the early books of the Bible, and, below the transom, eighty-one panels based on the last book, *Revelations*, altogether forming an extensive monumental Apocalypse cycle. The Old Testament panels, with themes of light and darkness and good and evil, were chosen as prefigurations of the Last Judgement at the end of time. The panels of the bottom row, in which the donor, Bishop Skirlaw of Durham, is flanked by twenty-four legendary and historic kings and ecclesiastics associated with York (themselves prefiguring the twenty-four elders of the Apocalypse), place the city

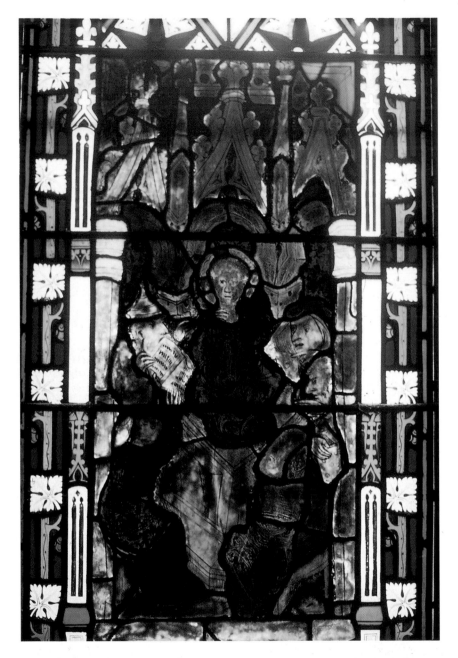

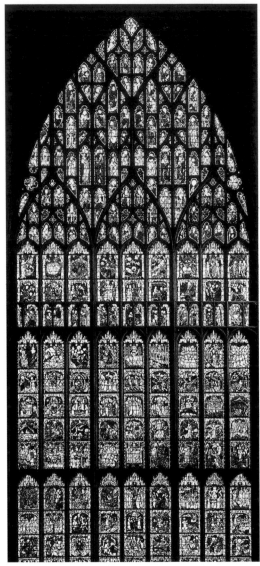

7 Christ disputing with the doctors in the Temple, part of a window of *c.*1420 from the Judenburg area of Austria but now in St John's Church, Kirkby Wharfe, Yorkshire. The medieval glass is extremely heavily corroded unlike the nineteenth-century surrounds.

8 With its elaborate combination of Old Testament and Apocalypse subjects, the east window of York Minster acts as a huge altarpiece in glass dominating the choir of the Cathedral.

and its Cathedral firmly within this vision of history. When the author of *Revelations* describes the descent of the Heavenly Jerusalem, an event depicted towards the bottom right of the window, he does so in terms of an architecture of precious stones, transparent glass and light: 'And the city had no need of the sun, neither of the moon, to shine in it: for the glory of God did lighten it, and the Lamb is the light thereof'. These passages would have been sung at the service of dedication held to mark the rebuilding of the Gothic Cathedral.

Medieval men and women were used to seeking meaning in shadows, signs and symbols, and the artists who worked on this window exploited symbolism in a number of ways, most obviously in the typological linking of Old and New Testament themes. The daily miracle of light and darkness had special significance for a window concerned with good and evil, and the York work with its transparent wall of jewel-like colour, was peculiarly suited to reinforce in visual terms the idea that the newly completed choir of the Cathedral could be interpreted as symbolising the Heavenly Jerusalem here on earth.

John Thornton's role in devising the iconographic programme is not known; it appears to be the product of a theologically trained mind and forms part of a larger glazing scheme in the choir to promote the cult of local saints and proclaim the history of Christianity in northern England. His creative intervention and imaginative response to the challenge of such a complex series of images cannot, however, be denied. He skilfully edited the 'text' so that certain key scenes containing God were placed centrally in the window, and, mindful of the distance of certain panels from the eye, he modified traditional forms of representation to make designs more· legible from the floor. Events and characters are depicted with a feel for psychology and drama and the individual panels are designed and painted with a wealth of detail and brilliance of technique which cannot possibly be appreciated from ground level.

According to the contract, Thornton was responsible for designing the east window and for painting some of the glass. It was not the product, then, of an individual genius but the work of a team of glaziers of whom only the master in charge is known. This vast project

9, 10 St John's Vision of Christ and the Candlesticks (see *Revelations* 1) depicted in the east window of York Minster (left), is based on earlier manuscript traditions represented here by a page from the Lambeth Apocalypse (right), probably illuminated in London *c*.1260–7. According to the biblical text the seven stars should be in Christ's hand but the designer of the glass has enlarged them and placed them on the left against a dark background so that they are more clearly visible from ground level.

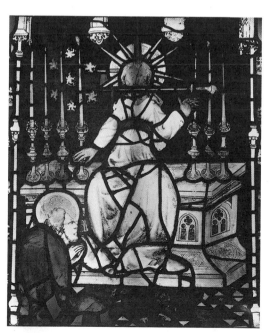

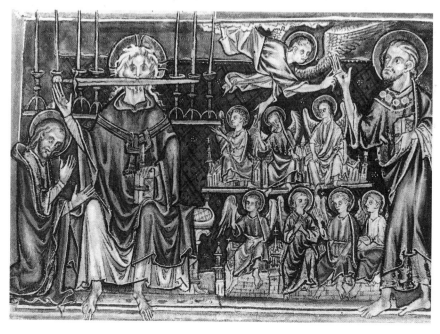

11 The Register of Freemen in York, listing those craftsmen admitted to the freedom in 1410. Among them is John Thornton (Johannes Thornton Glasyer), the third entry here.

took only three years to complete and Thornton's organisational skills seem remarkable when it is remembered that it took the Minster glaziers, admittedly not such a large body of men, over ten years to reorganise and relead the window after it returned from wartime storage earlier this century. Had Thornton worked in any other medium but glass-painting he would probably be regarded as a major English artist.

Thornton was responsible for one of the few medieval windows in the whole of York Minster for which the name of a glazier is known. He came from Coventry in Warwickshire to glaze the most prestigious window in the north of England, and remained in York, becoming a Freeman of the City in 1410, where he is last heard of in 1433 when the Dean and Chapter made a payment to him.

A document shows that he still retained property in Coventry at St John's Bridges in 1413, so it is possible that he ran workshops in both cities, and it is interesting that on the basis of stylistic analysis a number of windows both in York and elsewhere in the north of England, as well as in Great Malvern and the Midlands, has been ascribed to his workshop. The only firmly documented window on which he worked is the York Minster east window, for which a seventeenth-century transcript of the original contract exists, as well as Thornton's badly damaged monogram in the glass, a rare feature in a medieval window. All this amounts to little evidence from which to construct an artist's career, although it is a great deal more than is normal for a medieval glass-painter. All kinds of information which would be desirable — for example, on Thornton's training, his intellectual background, the way that he organised his workshops, the visual sources he drew on — remain largely hidden.

Problems of terminology dog any consideration of the medieval glass-painter. Words and the concepts they express change in the course of time. During the Middle Ages the term commonly used for those working on window glass, at least in documents, was the Latin *vitriarius*, French *verrier* or *verrour* and, from the fourteenth century, the English *glazenwright* or *glazier*, though the latter was also used initially for someone who actually manufactured glass. All these terms emphasise the medium itself and embrace all aspects of window production; rarely does the separate sphere of the glass-painter receive any stress: for example, Magister Fridericus (Master Friedrich), *vitriarius pictor*, who worked at the Abbey of Klosterneuberg in Austria during the second half of the thirteenth century, was probably both a glazier and a painter, rather than a glass-painter. With the increasing divide between the craft and artistic elements in window production during the course of the sixteenth century, the word *glazier* became more specialised and was reserved for those making leaded lights, with its pejorative associations of being allied to plumbing (that is, working in lead), while terms like *glass-painter* and *peintre-verrier* were coined for those of more artistic bent who worked on stained glass windows. This division is nicely represented in visual terms in the two woodcuts, one representing the glazier and the other the glass-painter, included in Jost Amman's *Panoplia Omnium Artium*, printed in Frankfurt in 1568.

The changes in terminology more or less coincide with the beginnings of the decline of stained glass as a major art form. The Victorian stained glass historian Charles Winston appealed in his *Memoirs Illustrative of the Art of Glass-Painting* (1855) to 'the professors of the noblest arts, in favour of this unhappy art of glass-painting. It is impossible to look at the glass of Chartres, Angers or Brussels, without feeling that glass-painting was once practised by artists'. He was attempting to rescue the medium, which he saw at the time of the Gothic Revival of the nineteenth century as dominated by 'glasswrights' and tradesmen. William Morris (1834–96) and his associates, and their followers in the Arts and Crafts Movement, did much to rectify the situation in Britain, trying to integrate designer and executant and achieve a unity which had not been seen since the end of the Middle Ages. The division between art and craft can still be an issue amongst those working in stained glass today.

It was not only nineteenth-century artists and historians who looked to the period before the Renaissance as a golden age of glass-painting:

12 Woodcuts of *The Glazier* (left) and *The Glass-Painter* (right) from the Zürich artist Jost Amman's *Panoplia Omnium Artium* (Book of Trades) published in Frankfurt in 1568. In the glazier's workshop, where a panel of bull's eye glass is being leaded up, various tools can be seen, including grozing irons, soldering irons and a lead mill. The glass-painter is shown at work in a well lit studio painting a small-scale panel for which the design hangs to his left. Cartoons for domestic and heraldic panels also hang on the wall.

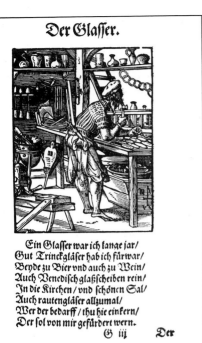

Der Glaffer.

Ein Glaffer war ich lange jar/
Gut Trinckgläfer hab ich fürwar/
Beyde zu Bier vnd auch zu Wein/
Auch Venedifch glaßfcheiben rein/
In die Kirchen/ vnd fchönen Sal/
Auch rautengläfer allzumal/
Wer der bedarff/ thu hie einkern/
Der fol von mir gefürdert wern.
G iij   Der

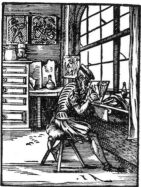

Der Glaßmaler.

Einen Glaßmaler heißt man mich/
In die Gläfer kan fchmeltzen ich/
Bildwerck/ manch herrliche Perfon/
Adelich Frauwen vnde Mann/
Sampt jren Kindern abgebild/
Vnd jres gfchlechts Wappen vnd Schilt/
Daß man erkennen kan darbey/
Wann diß Gefchlecht herkommen fey.
                              Der

for those with strong religious convictions the windows of the Gothic cathedral were products of an age of faith. Given these historical circumstances it is not surprising that something of the mystery and mystique of the windows themselves became transferred to those who had made them. But today we too approach the medieval glass-painter with all kinds of preconceptions.

Like other medieval artists and artisans, glass-painters were not a class apart: they were paid professionals with specific tasks to carry out and they worked to commission. Medieval documents show the glazier as part of a team of practical building workers, along with masons, carpenters and smiths. Their primary role was to work with glass, but the architectural nature of the tasks they performed meant that they might be called on to point a window, prepare the glazing grooves in a window prior to fixing the glass, or help with the iron *ferramenta* which supported the glass in its framework. Occasionally more complex jobs might be carried out with stonework, as for example in 1540 when the Parisian glass-painter Jacques Vignant fixed

a stone mullion before installing a window in the church of Saint-Germain at Nozay (Essonne).

Because of the nature of the processes which had to be carried out when making a stained glass window – cutting, firing, leading and so on (see Chapter 5) – craft skills were as important as artistic ability for the small workshops which were the norm during the Middle Ages. Division of labour was used as a means of organising very large commissions, but even then separation between the artist or designer and the craftsmen who executed the work seems to have been much less common than it became later on. John de Chester, the master glazier in 1351–2 at St Stephen's Chapel, Westminster, was paid both for designing and painting glass, as was John Thornton in York. In Italy, where panel- and fresco-painting were predominant, it was much more common for wealthy patrons to turn to major artists like Andrea del Castagno or Paolo Uccello for window designs. The late fourteenth-century Florentine painter, Cennino Cennini, was scornful of those who worked on stained glass: 'It is true that the occupation is not much practised by our profession and is practised more by those who make a business of it. And ordinarily those masters who do the work possess more skill than draftsmanship, and they are almost forced to turn, for help on the drawings, to someone who possesses finished craftsmanship, that is, to one of all-round, good ability'. Designing the cartoons and painting the glass were regarded as the provinces of the painter, and what might be seen as the more mechanical aspects of production were to be carried out by someone less talented.

North of the Alps, too, a special patron on occasion used a favourite artist in his employ to design stained glass. For example, Peter the Painter whitewashed windows and walls and drew masonry lines and roses on them at the royal castle at Marlborough, Wiltshire, in 1237 and he also made a window there. Glaziers might sometimes work in other media, like Master John who repaired the canopy of Edward I's bed at Westminster Palace in 1287; but because of guild structures they were not normally encouraged to work in more than one specific craft.

Not only did the individual glazier's tasks vary, but so did the glazing work in the workshop. Prestigious stained glass windows for halls, palaces and great churches were produced alongside plain glazing, like that for Henry III's latrine in the royal hunting lodge of Clipstone, Nottinghamshire, in 1252, or the window for a pigeon loft for Peterhouse, Cambridge, on the College's estate at Thriplow in 1441.

Besides designing and making new windows, medieval glaziers and glass-painters were frequently employed to maintain and repair existing work, an aspect of the craft which has not received the attention it deserves, despite plentiful documentation in medieval records. Stained glass windows can be remarkably resilient, but they do need regular attention and care. Problems can arise at any stage in their manufacture: the glass itself can corrode, paint can flake off and lead decay. If the stonework or ironwork supporting the panels falls into disrepair, damage can occur to the glass.

The Fabric Rolls of York Minster which survive from the fourteenth century onwards,

contain regular entries for repairs to windows by local workshops. Documents at Chartres for the period 1415—16 record payments of large sums of money for glass, lead, charcoal and premises for the glaziers used during a restoration of the famous twelfth- and thirteenth-century windows. During recent work on the three windows at the west end of the nave, the glass historian Françoise Perrot produced charts to show the extent of previous restorations of the glass. During the Middle Ages there was little concern for historical authenticity, and hence no purist approach to restoration works. If pieces of glass were missing, a glass-painter was brought in to maintain the aesthetic integrity of the work. The late medieval glass-painters who worked at Chartres responded to the styles and techniques of their predecessors, as the figure of Zephaniah from the Jesse Tree [13] shows. The fifteenth-century restorer who replaced the head, adapted his normal approach to fit in with the more stylised drawing of the original mid twelfth-century artist, one small example of what the glass historian Madeline Caviness has called a 'conservationist trend and an attitude of respect for ancient works' in medieval stained glass.

It is not surprising to find concern about maintenance of windows when glass was such a costly and valuable commodity. Abbot Suger, who described the windows he had commissioned for the new east end at Saint-Denis, constructed around 1140 to 1144, illustrates the point well:

Now because they are very valuable on account of their wonderful execution and the profuse expenditure of painted glass and sapphire glass, we appointed an official master craftsman for their protection and repair and also a skilled goldsmith for the gold and silver ornaments, and who would receive their allowances and what was adjudged them in addition, that is coins from the altar and flour from the common storehouse of the brethren, and who would never neglect their duty to look after these things.

About a century later another great patron, Louis IX, made similar arrangements at the Sainte-Chapelle in Paris, and in 1240 John the Glazier and his heirs were appointed to maintain the windows of Chichester Cathedral for a daily supply of bread and an annual fee of one mark:

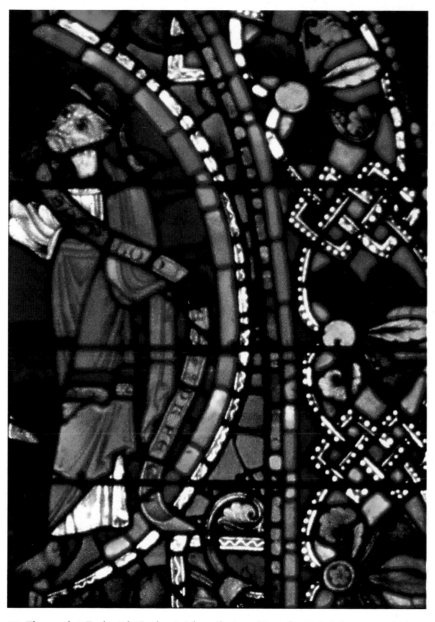

13 The prophet Zephaniah (Sophonias) from the Jesse Tree of *c.*1150 at the west end of Chartres Cathedral. A replacement head was painted in the early fifteenth century but the restorer attempted to match the style of the original glass.

They shall preserve the ancient glass windows, and what has to be washed and cleaned they shall wash and clean, and what has to be repaired they shall repair, at the cost of the church, and what has to be added they shall add, likewise at the cost of the church, and there shall be allowed them for each foot of addition one penny.

Medieval accounts do occasionally contain very specific payments for restoration work. Thomas of Oxford's late fourteenth-century figures of Amos and Samuel from the Jesse Tree at Winchester College were repaired by Stephen Glasyer in 1457 at a substantial cost of one mark (13s. 4d.), and his contemporary John Prudde, was paid a shilling for each of the 'two heads of virgins broken' and 6d. for each of the 'two vestments, one of a bishop, the other of a virgin', when he was working at Greenwich Palace.

Glaziers could also be asked to salvage old glass for reuse in a new window. For the chapel glazing at the Tower of London in 1286 some new glass was purchased but 8s. 4d. was also paid 'for 40 feet of old glass made up and renewed at $2\frac{1}{2}$d. a foot'. Such reuse of old glass may have been more common than is realised as it is usually difficult to identify today.

The careful preservation of individual panels, or whole series of panels, for reglazing in later buildings may be ascribed not only to the expense of cost, but also to religious or even aesthetic considerations. The most famous example of this practice is the image of the Virgin and Child, known as *La Belle-Verrière* at 14 Chartres. The three main panels date from about 1180 and miraculously survived the fire which destroyed most of the Cathedral in 1194. Because it was a famous devotional image, the restored glass was placed in thirteenth-century surrounds and re-erected in the south choir aisle of the Cathedral. At Strasbourg at the end of the thirteenth century, a series of German emperors dating from around 1200, originally in the high windows of the Romanesque nave, was reused along with new figures in the style of the old in the lower windows of the new Gothic nave. At York several late twelfth-century panels of biblical scenes, lives of the saints and the Last Judgement, were preserved from the windows of the Romanesque Cathedral and set high up in the clerestory of the late thirteenth-century

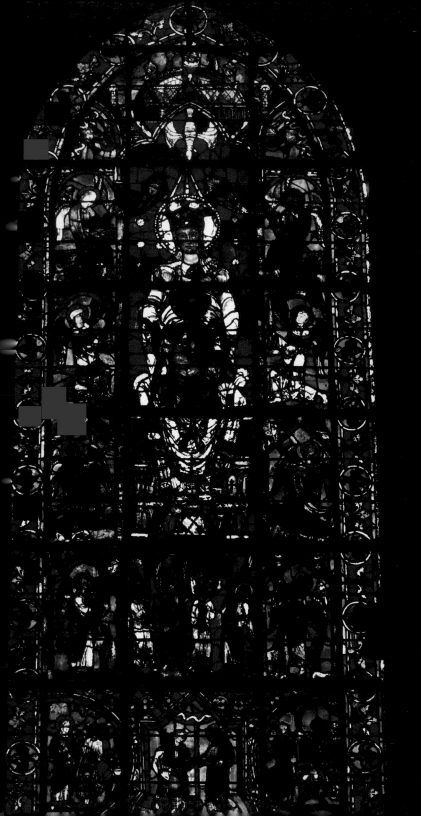

Gothic nave where they could not be seen too closely. This was an important aesthetic decision to make because the small scale of the panels and their intense colouring directly influenced the new panels that were made to go with them. As a result the nave of York Minster is rather unusual in having small figure-panels at clerestory level rather than the more usual monumental single figures of cathedrals like Bourges, Chartres or Cologne.

In a medium slow to change and traditional in its techniques it is not surprising to find some sympathy with the past. Exceptional examples of the glass-painter's art were preserved in the Middle Ages because of their outstanding artistic merit despite changes in fashion – the series of prophets at Augsburg of about 1100, the technically brilliant Redemption window of about 1147 at Châlons-sur-Marne, reused in the Cathedral after the fire of 1230, or the panels from a Jesse window and St Francis window of about 1235–45 reused in the Franciscan Barefoot Church at Erfurt in Germany in the early years of the fourteenth century.

This chapter began with a question about artists and craftsmen which, in the Middle Ages, could probably never have been asked. At that time, stained glass was a costly and prestigious art form and the materials and the skill which went into its creation were greatly valued. During the course of the sixteenth century the integration of the production of stained glass windows fragmented into distinct specialisations. Today, a glazier, or a stained glass artist, or a conservator, is called in; the medieval glass-painter combined aspects of all three.

14 The image of the Virgin and Child known as *La Belle-Verrière* from the choir of Chartres Cathedral. Glass of *c.*1180 which survived the fire of 1194 was reused in the early thirteenth-century church.

3 STATUS AND ORGANISATION

When studying medieval stained glass windows, it is often easier to identify the patron of a window than it is to find its artist, since donor portraits are relatively plentiful while images of glass-painters are rare. Artists received little public credit for their creativity and are usually only acknowledged in the prosaic documentation of financial transactions. In the relationship between the medieval artist and patron, it was the person who paid whose importance was paramount. Like the vast majority of medieval artists, the glass-painter tends to remain anonymous.

An early exception to this general rule is the glass-painter seen in a panel of about 1160 portraying Moses and the Burning Bush, from the Premonstratensian monastery of Arnstein, now in the Landesmuseum in Munster in West-

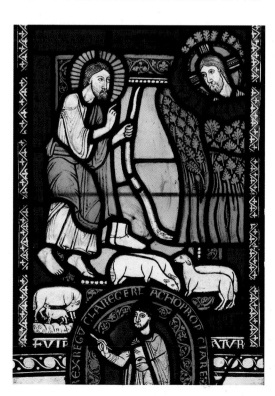

15 The glass-painter Gerlachus, depicted at the base of this panel, led a workshop responsible for five typological windows destined for the choir of the Abbey of Arnstein. Of the Old Testament scenes, only five, including this one of Moses and the Burning Bush, survive.

phalia. It depicts Gerlachus holding his brush and paint-pot and praying for the gift of light. A signature rather than a portrait can be seen in the Joseph window of about 1235 from the ambulatory of Rouen Cathedral, which refers to the otherwise unknown glass-painter Clement of Chartres. Evidence for their undoubted social status and economic prominence become more plentiful only in the late Middle Ages when artists emerge from historical obscurity. In the late 1380s, the Oxford glass-painter Thomas Glazier is described dining in hall with the scholars of New College. New College Chapel glazing was just one of a number of commissions that Thomas undertook for the wealthy and powerful William of Wykeham, Bishop of Winchester (1366–1404) and Chancellor of England (1367–71). In the east window of Winchester College Chapel, Wykeham's other great undertaking, a portrait of Thomas appears with the carpenter who is not named, William Wynford, the Master Mason and Master Simon Membury, Wykeham's clerk of works. (All were unfortunately replaced by careful copies in the nineteenth century.) The craftsmen and administrator (clerk of works) are in august company, for the outer base lights, albeit on a larger scale, contain figures of Wykeham himself and Kings Edward III and Richard II. Thomas' prosperous dress sets him on a par with his companions and a label bears the proud words *Thomas operator istius vitri*, (Thomas maker of this glass). Wykeham clearly appreciated the expertise of the craftsmen in his employ.

Two other portraits of English glass-painters are known, both from the early sixteenth century: first that of John Petty in York Minster, though now lost, is recorded in a seventeenth-century drawing, and second that of Ralph Harries at St Neot's in Cornwall. In each instance, the glass-painter was both artist and donor, which in itself reflects the growing social and economic status of some craftsmen in the late Middle Ages. Of a slightly later date is the self-portrait of the Beauvais glass-painter

16 The Joseph Window in Rouen Cathedral was the gift of the cloth merchants and contains the rare signature of a thirteenth-century French glass-painter, on the banderole held by the seated figure. The inscription reads *Clemens Vitrearius Carnotensis M[e Fecit]*, Clement, glass-painter of Chartres made me.

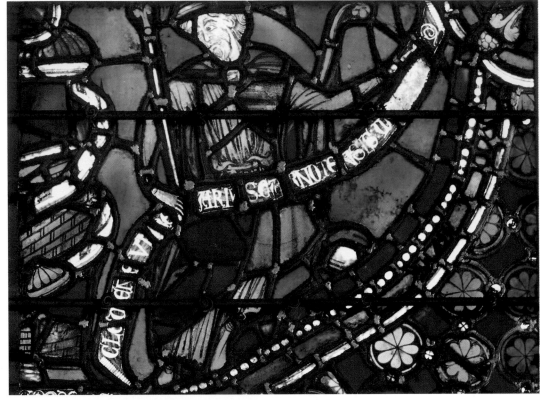

17 *Right* Dwarfed by the slippers of the sleeping Jesse, the Oxford glass-painter Thomas Glazier kneels in an attitude of prayer. Although the actual glass of the figure was replaced in the early nineteenth century, the copy is known to be extremely faithful to the original, and the cropped hair and distinctive whiskers suggest an element of real portraiture.

18 *Far right* The seventeenth-century antiquarian Henry Johnston wrote detailed notes, now in the Bodleian Library in Oxford, in which is preserved an annotated sketch of the portrait of the York master glazier, John Petty, formerly in glass in the south transept of York Minster.

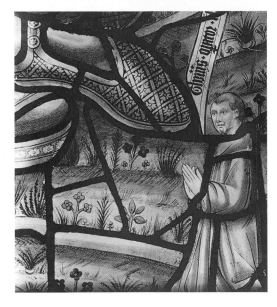

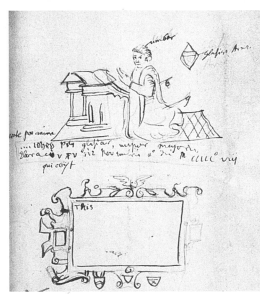

19 Engrand Le Prince, identifiable by the initials ENGR on his sleeve, and whose bearded face features in the sumptuous Jesse Tree in the church of St Etienne. Almost nothing is known of Engrand or his three talented brothers, Jean, Nicholas and Pierre, except that Engrand died in 1531.

In the late Middle Ages it became more common for glass-painters to sign or initial their work. The east window of York Minster, glazed between 1405 and 1408, for example, has at its apex the monogram of the glass-painter John Thornton and the sixteenth-century Metz glass-painter Valentin Busch initialled his windows with the monogram VB.

Although Theophilus, the twelfth-century author of the most important treatise on glass-painting, *De Diversis Artibus*, describes himself as 'priest and monk', there is no substantial evidence to suggest that the craft of glass-painting was widely practised in the cloister. However, one monk Daniel, who died in 1155, is described as *vitrearius* of the Abbey of St Benet at Holme in Norfolk, where he is said to have made the windows in the church, and some royal accounts of 1278 refer to a Cistercian monk of Pipewell in Northamptonshire who made windows for Rockingham Castle. In both cases it is likely that the monks had acquired their skills before entering the religious life. Daniel at least appears to have had a wife and son before retiring to the monastery. In the twelfth century, Abbot Suger of Saint-Denis employed a glazier to maintain and repair the Abbey windows, which suggests that glazing skills were not available amongst the monks. In thirteenth-century Austria there is evidence that glass-painters sometimes entered a monastic community as lay brothers, living on the fringe of the religious community; Master Friedrich and his son Master Walther achieved this status at Klosterneuburg. One notable exception to this trend was the French glass-painter Guillaume de Marcillat, who entered the Dominican house in Nevers before departing to work at the Vatican in 1506. Three years later he was granted papal permission to leave his order and become a regular canon of the Augustinians.

Documentary evidence of glass-painters and their activities is plentiful, but although many hundreds of craftsmen are named, particularly in financial accounts, very few of their windows can now be identified. The records show that many large English towns supported groups of glass-painters, who by the early thirteenth century had become organised into an urban craft group. Glass-painters employed in the 1350s at St Stephen's Chapel, Westminster, had been summoned by writs issued to twenty-seven counties. Indeed, their names confirm their wide geographical origins — John de Chester, John Lincoln, William Lichfield, Robert Norwich and William Hereford, to name but a few. Oxford has already been mentioned as a centre, and in the second half of the fifteenth century, other Midland towns such as Stamford, Peterborough and Burton-on-Trent all sustained important workshops. In East Anglia, Norwich and King's Lynn were prominent in the fifteenth century and recent research has now established

19 In a window characterised by the brilliance of its technique is preserved the ruddy-haired, bare-headed portrait of its author, Engrand le Prince.

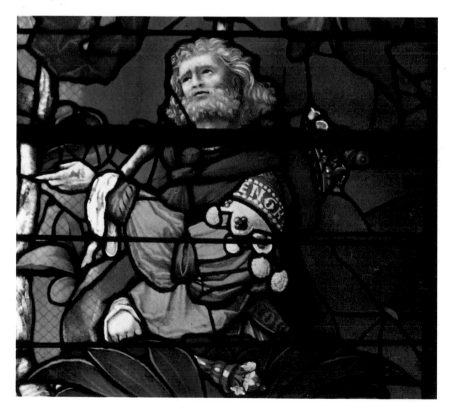

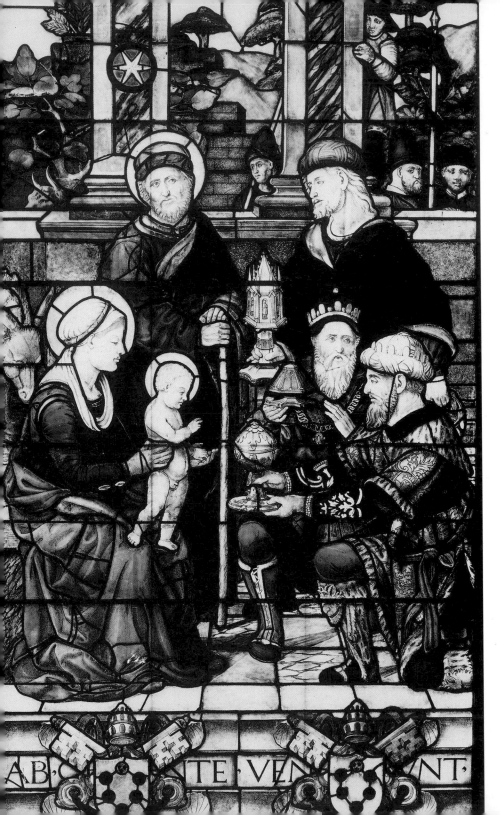

Exeter in Devon as a significant centre in the fourteenth century. That Coventry was a flourishing centre of the craft can be inferred from its remaining stained glass and from the fact that it was to this city that the Dean and Chapter of York turned when they sought a master to glaze the east window of the Minster. The records of glass-painters for the city of York are amongst the most extensive and best studied of the English documents. Between 1313 and 1555 over one hundred glaziers and glass-painters can be identified in the Freemen's Registers, while over roughly the same period, more than fifty names appear in the Norwich records.

Glass-painting was well established in French towns at an early date. Abbot Suger describes how the sumptuous windows of the 1140s at Saint-Denis were created by glass-painters from many regions. By the fifteenth century, large glass-painting communities had been established in Beauvais, Rouen, Troyes, Dijon, Toulouse, Avignon, Marseille, Lyons and, of course, Paris. The Rhineland was an early centre of glass-painting and it is no surprise that Theophilus emerged from there. By the fourteenth and fifteenth centuries, cities such as Freiburg, Nuremberg, Ulm, Esslingen, Erfurt and Strasbourg, all had flourishing glazing communities.

As discussed above, the interpretation of the terminology used to describe those people carrying out glazing work can be problematic. Can the man called 'glazier' and paid a few pence have fulfilled the same role as the master employed to paint and install a complete glazing scheme? For most of the Middle Ages, the various names used to describe glass-painters and glaziers appear to have been used interchangeably and indiscriminately and the small quantity of positive evidence available suggests that there was no substantial separation of the simple glazing and more complex stained glass crafts. The Norwich man, Nicholas Peyntor, Glazier, mentioned in 1481, can perhaps be confidently identified as a painter of glass, but it is debatable to what extent the modern concept of the separation of glass-painting and glazing had any real meaning in the Middle Ages. In the

Opposite This window from Cortona Cathedral by Guillaume de Marcillat was erected in 1516 as a gift from Pope Leo x, Giovanni de Medici, whose arms appear at the foot of the panel.

Norwich records of 1457, Master Thomas Goldbeater's workshop contained two apprentice glaziers, John Thompson and William Heyward, and one apprentice painter, Richard Steere. By 1505, William Heyward had become an independent master and was taking on apprentices of his own. Theophilus' treatise implies that all aspects of the creation of a window were unified within one workshop, although the extent to which individuals executed every operation no doubt depended on expertise and talent. It would seem that even the grandest workshops accepted relatively lowly glazing commissions.

Only late in the Middle Ages is there any evidence of a degree of specialisation that caused the roles of 'glazier' and 'glass-painter', the creator of stained glass windows, to be separated. In part, this can probably be attributed to the increasing demand for domestic glazing – in 1533, twenty-one feet of ready-cut quarries (diamond-shaped pieces of glass) were bought at Durham and no doubt required relatively little specialised skill to install them. It is also in the late fifteenth and the sixteenth centuries that the term 'glass-painter' is first encountered.

Having looked at the evidence for the status of the glass-painter, how the craft was organised will now be considered. Throughout the Middle Ages the practice of every craft was regulated by the guild system upheld by the civic authority of the mayor and aldermen or their equivalents, a system which served to protect the interests of craftsman and patron alike. Guilds of glass-painters are known to have existed in London, Chester, Norwich and York. The earliest surviving English regulations are those from London, dating from 1364/5, and the York Ordinances surviving from about 1380 and 1463/4. It is from these regulations that we gain some insight into the organisation of the craft and the way in which its practitioners were trained, although the ordinances are silent on many issues, and day-to-day practices must have depended on long-established traditions. The York Ordinances decreed that all work done above the value of half a mark should be inspected by the Guild's *serchours* ('searchers',

master glaziers appointed by a guild to maintain standards) before it left the city, an order clearly intended to safeguard the reputation of York craftsmanship – sharp practices, such as the use of unfired paint, quick, easy but impermanent, would easily be spotted by the expert searchers. *The Ordinances of the York Glaziers* of 1463/4 are specific about this: 'They shall emonges hem selfe every yere in the fest of Seint Luke chese hem two that shall be made in the said craft, and to see that it be wele, truely, and substancially wroght, and that therein be noo disceyt unto the kynges peple'. The statutes of the Paris glaziers of 1467 and the Lyons glass-painters confirmed by King Charles VIII in 1496, are very precise about tasks to be undertaken and stress at length the quality of the materials to be used and the craft skills of the glaziers. Severe penalties were stipulated for malpractice or sub-standard workmanship.

The guild regulated admission to the practice of its craft. To quote the York Ordinances, no one could 'sett up a shop as a master unto suche tyme he aggre with the serchours of the said craft for a certain some'. The searchers were appointed annually on the Feast of St Luke, who was himself believed to have been a painter and therefore a saint to whom medieval artists and particularly painters were universally devoted, and to whom many medieval painters' guilds were dedicated. The Norwich glass-painters, unlike their York and London brethren, did not have their own guild, but were members, together with the bell-founders, braisers, painters, pewterers and plumbers, of the Guild of St Luke. In Prague in 1365, the glass-painters joined with other artists in St Luke's Guild, while in fifteenth-century Paris, the glass-painters joined with the painters, sculptors and embroiderers. In sixteenth-century Antwerp, glass-painters, Dirck Vellert for example, belonged to the Guild of St Luke. The unspecified admission fee mentioned in the York records could no doubt be set to discourage the establishment of inadequately financed ventures and would naturally concentrate the craft in the hands of a few well-funded workshops. Training, which seems usually to have begun at the age of ten, was given only in the milieu of the workshop

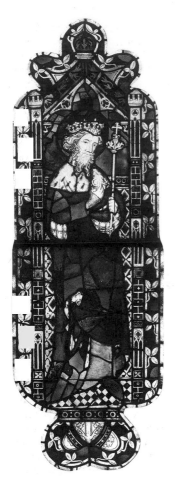

21 St Edward the Confessor is one of the four figures executed by Robert Lyen for the Dean and Chapter of Exeter in 1391. He was paid 1s. 8d. for every square foot of new glass he supplied to the reconstructed east window.

and lasted for a number of years – four, seven or even ten. In England, where seven years of training was preferred, apprentices could be taken on only one at a time, and a second one only when the first had completed four years training. In many countries an apprentice was sometimes required to submit a special panel of glass known as a 'master-piece' as evidence of his proficiency – this might include difficult cutting or the drilling of a piece of glass to receive a 'jewel'. The fifteenth-century Vienna Ordinances stipulated that for such a master-piece 'a glazier shall design and paint a panel of glass work'. By restricting the numbers of apprentices employed by a single master, the guilds could prevent the market being flooded by half-trained craftsmen, and the skilled and qualified artist acquired a considerable cachet. Infringement of any of the guild's regulations carried stiff fines – in York the maximum fine for most infringements was one mark.

The guilds guarded their jurisdiction jealously. Most medieval cities included a number of liberties, areas belonging to a castle or monastery, for example, whose residents were bound by their own laws, free from overall civic control. In York the glass-painters' Guild would have come into contact with other artists working within the liberty of St Peter, which included the Minster itself. Only in 1410 did John Thornton become a freeman of the city and an independent master in his own right; this was not necessary as long as he remained solely in the employ of the Dean and Chapter. In late fifteenth-century London those glass-painters wishing to elude the jurisdiction of the Glaziers' Guild resided in Southwark, beyond the city boundary.

The practice of limiting apprentices suggests that workshops were generally quite small – a master and a few assistants at different stages of training and experience – and other documentary sources reinforce the idea. In Exeter in 1391 the Cathedral records mention only Robert Lyen and an assistant working on the east window – presumably unqualified apprentices did not rate a separate mention. For the glazing of the great east window, the Dean and Chapter of York employed John Thornton and specified

that he was to take on workmen, *operarios*, to assist with the work, which was to be completed within three years. That it was necessary to make this specific provision for additional assistance suggests that Thornton's normal team was insufficient for this exceptional commission. A recently discovered letter patent of 1497 enrolled in the register of the Bishop of Durham, relates to the appointment of the King's Glazier and confirms this picture of workshop size. Barnard Flower, probably a native of the Netherlands but resident in Southwark, was appointed while working at the royal palace at Shene, and was authorised to maintain a workshop of three or four men. When Robert Preston of York died in 1503 his will instructed that his tools be equally divided between his three apprentices.

The invaluable accounts for the glazing in 22 1351–2 of St Stephen's Chapel, Westminster, mirror in the scale of their payments both the division of labour within a workshop and the varying levels of skill present in any one group of craftsmen. Master glaziers received a shilling per day, while ordinary glaziers earned only 6d. or 7d. and their assistants a meagre 4d. or $4\frac{1}{2}$d. The accounts also make it clear that the role of the master was to design and cartoon the windows, tracing the full-scale design onto the whitewashed tables on which the other glaziers were to work.

The size of the St Stephen's workshop was unprecedented, however, owing both to the size and complexity of the commission and the speed with which the scheme was to be completed. When faced with large commissions, an alternative to the creation of an exceptionally large single workshop was for two workshops to join forces, as in the glazing of the west wall of York Minster in about 1339. Archbishop Melton commissioned Master Robert to glaze the west window, while a second master, Thomas Bouesdon, working in an almost indistinguishable style, was involved in the provision of the flanking aisle windows. Whether this partnership was decided by patron or artists is impossible to say. At Berne Minster in 1447, the local Magerfitz workshop had to collaborate with an outsider, Meister Bernhard.

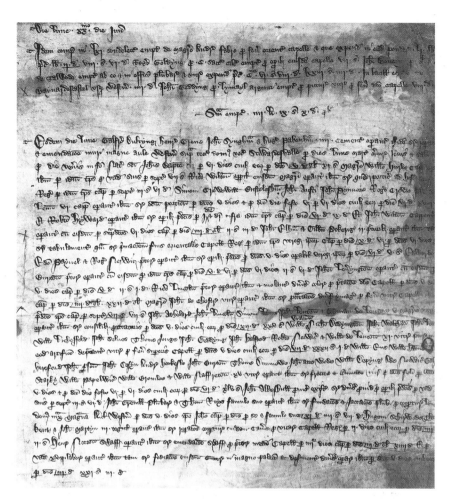

22 An extract from the accounts for the glazing of St Stephen's Chapel, Westminster, for Monday 20 June 1351.

produced white glass, manufactured in Kent, Sussex, Surrey and Staffordshire, was best transported by water. York glaziers purchased most of their sheets of coloured glass from the Rhineland and the Rouen area, through the Hanse warehouses in Hull and thence up the River Ouse. In London the River Thames was crucial – French glass was off-loaded at the bottom of Thames Street, near London Bridge. The present-day Glaziers' Hall is still located next to London Bridge, but on the opposite side of the River. In contrast to this geographic concentration, and possibly to be explained by the variety of sources for their raw materials, Parisian glass-painters are to be found living and working throughout the city; in 1297 seventeen glass-painters are found living in ten different parishes.

Despite the difficulties in transporting bulky and weighty items – a panel of stained glass held together by lead is a heavy object – it is clear that in most cases very little work other than the fixing was done on site. In 1322 John de Walworth supplied a number of plain glass windows to Westminster Palace and payments were made for land and water transport 'from Kandelwekstrete [Cannon Street] to Westminster'. In 1353 figured windows for Carisbrooke Castle were transported from Winchester. From 1351–2 the St Stephen's Chapel workshop made a series of windows for Windsor Castle. Boards and nails were purchased for the construction of the packing cases, with 14d. worth of hay and straw to provide cushioning for the panels. The Thames provided the means of transport, at a cost of 4s. The journey in 1393 from the workshop of Thomas Glazier in Oxford to Winchester College was undertaken by cart and was consequently more expensive, costing 19s. 3d.

Very few small or rural communities would have boasted a glazing shop in their midst. The parish churches and wealthier householders would have to turn to the local town for glazing repairs and maintenance and had to be prepared to cover the glass-painter's expenses when estimating, measuring for templates and fixing, as well as the actual glazing costs. In 1527 the church wardens of Tilney All Saints in Norfolk

Glass-painters' businesses, like those of other professions, were often concentrated in particular parishes. In York, Stonegate was the street in which a number of them resided and in the fifteenth century at least ten of them were buried in the church of St Helen at the south end of Stonegate. A further three were buried in St Michael-le-Belfrey at the opposite end of the street. In York and Norwich, the glass-painting community was to be found living in areas between the cathedral, their major patron, and the river, underlining the importance of water transport, both for the easy importation of the coloured glasses made on the Continent and for the moving of completed windows. Even home-

paid 9s. 3d. 'to Robert Nobylles wyffe for bordyng of ye forseid glasers' and 8d. for 'ye glasers dyner ye fyrst day'.

The most prestigious appointment in the English profession was that of King's Glazier, a post that enjoyed particular privileges. The master glass-painter Edward is described as 'chief glazier' to Henry III at Windsor in 1242. Although a number of other glaziers worked for Kings Edward I, II and III at Westminster and elsewhere, there is no documentary evidence for an official post of King's Glazier until 1378 when John de Brampton, Master of the London Glaziers' Company in 1373, was appointed 'King's Glazier within the Tower of London, the palace of Westminster, and all his other castles and manors'. Richard Savage was appointed his successor for life in 1393 but was not on a regular salary. He was to 'receive for such time as he shall be employed on the king's glass works whatever shall be agreed between the Clerk of the King's Works and the said Richard'. It was not until 1412 that Roger Gloucester, Savage's successor, obtained a fee of 12d. a day. The best indication of the benefits of the post can be gleaned from the Patent Rolls of 1440, recording John Prudde's appointment in succession to Roger Gloucester. In addition to the salary and payments that Roger had enjoyed, Prudde was to have the customary use of 'a shedde called the glasyer logge' within Westminster Palace, and a gown of the King's livery every Christmas. The lodge was clearly a spacious and commodious place to work, measuring 60 ft by 20 ft (18.3 m by 6 m). The King's Glazier was not confined to work for the king: in addition to glazing the chapel at Eton College for Henry VI, Prudde also glazed the sumptuous Beauchamp Chapel in St Mary's Church at Warwick in 1447, although of his work for the King, nothing survives. References to packing materials suggests that Prudde executed his commissions in the lodge at Westminster, with the finished panels transported for installation.

At the same time as Richard II was creating the post of King's Glazier in England, Charles VI of France was instituting the similar post of *peintre du roi*. Glass-painters were so valued by Charles VI, that in 1390 he exempted them from

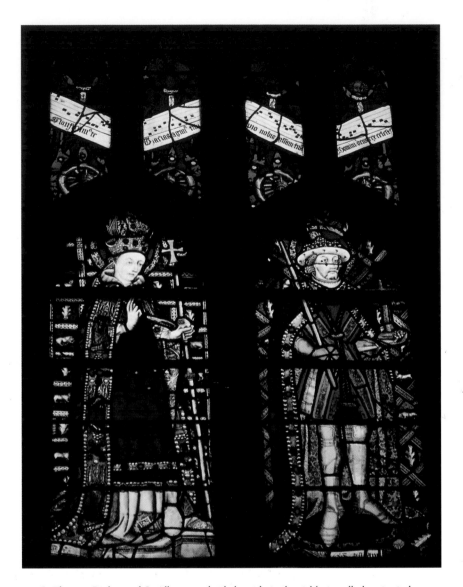

23 St Thomas Becket and St Alban stand side by side in the richly jewelled east window of the Beauchamp Chapel in St Mary's Church, Warwick, commissioned in 1447 and executed by the workshop of John Prudde, the King's Glazier. Note the jewels leaded into the hem of the robes and the mitre of St Thomas Becket.

taxes and subsidies, a privilege that was confirmed in 1430 by Charles VII and was renewed several times in the course of the sixteenth century.

Glass-painters were often active in the governance of their cities – Matthew le Verrer of Colchester was bailiff of the city (that is, chief magistrate) in 1313, 1332, 1337, 1349 and 1351, and in 1334 and 1338 he went to Parliament. Robert Preston (d.1503) and John Petty, both glass-painters of York, were members of the city's most prestigious religious confraternity, the Guild of Corpus Christi. Petty served as sheriff and alderman and in 1508 became the Lord Mayor of the city, dying in office. In Norwich, William Heyward became chamberlain in 1499. Nor was civic responsibility shirked by Continental glass-painters – Peter Hemmel, for example, served as municipal magistrate in Strasbourg in 1475–6.

That they were wealthy men can occasionally be seen from tax records. For example, the lay subsidy rolls for Yorkshire of 1327 record *Robertus le glasenwryght* (Master Robert perhaps) and *Agnes le glasenwryght*, two out of only nineteen people living in the parish of St Wilfrid in York who were rich enough to be assessed for tax. Further evidence of wealth is found in the wills of York glass-painters which mention luxury goods such as 'a small mazer set with silver' and six silver spoons, a 'hupe of gold' and an illuminated primer. John Petty listed 'a lityll covered cope bordered at fot wt [with] sylver and gilt', 'a great brass pot with the feet' and a 'standynge cup wt a cover gilt wt a egill of it'. The Norwich glass-painters had also attained considerable substance by the fifteenth century. Thomas Goldbeater, buried with his wife Katherine in the church of St Peter Parmentergate, is described as being 'a gentleman of coat armour'. Nicholas Peyntor, buried in 1504 in the churchyard of St George Colegate, had given £4 to the church to which he had already donated a window, and left 3s. 4d. for the repair of St Olave's Chapel. A second glazier, William Stalen was buried inside the church in 1513, before the image of St Peter, leaving 40s. towards the glazing. Valentin Busch, who originated in Strasbourg, was appointed in 1520 as

glass-painter to Metz Cathedral. When he died in 1541, among his possessions was an oil painting of the Virgin Mary and fourteen ounces of silver.

Although in most cities, Chester among them, a glass-painter was allowed to practise no other business, elsewhere this sort of restriction does not seem to have applied in certain circumstances to the practice of closely related skills. For example, in 1237 Peter the Painter made a window in Marlborough Castle and also whitewashed and decorated the surrounding walls. John Athelard is described as a master glass-painter in the accounts of St Stephen's Chapel and Windsor, but was entrusted with recruitment of wall-painters, with whom he also seems to have worked. A number of glass-painters are known to have kept inns, including Matthew of Colchester in 1310 and John Petty, who was forced to give it up when made an alderman of York in 1504.

There is even a little evidence that a number of women practised as glass-painters. Widows of masters often carried on their husband's business. For example, in 1542 the widow of the Paris glass-painter Jean Chastellain was paid for a window, and there are a number of instances of two businesses merging as the result of the remarriage of a glazier's widow – Peter Hemmel married the widow of a glazier in Strasbourg and acquired her husband's business. In sixteenth-century Paris, the widows of glass-painters tended to remarry other masters rather than their husband's assistants. Although in the past there has been a tendency to assume that women such as Agnes le glasenwryght were not practising craftswomen, but were merely continuing a family business, the presence of a small percentage of women in other related crafts suggests that Jehanne la verriere, Ysabellot la verriere, Edeline la verriere and a second Jehanne, all described in Parisian tax rolls between 1292 and 1313, may well have been practising glaziers. In the records of Troyes the name of Jeanne Coppin, wife of Henriet Coppin stands out. She is described as working with her husband, who died in 1482.

Once a year, glass-painters in English towns joined the other guilds in the public spectacle of the Corpus Christi pageants or mystery plays. In Norwich and York the glass-painters presented pageants requiring particular imagination and ingenuity; in York they performed *Jesus destroying Hell; twelve good and twelve evil spirits*, while in Norwich the pageant was *Hell Carte*, performed together with the stainers, scriveners, parchment-makers and the more practical gravers, colermakers and wheelwrights. In York, the glass-painters joined forces with the saddlers and fuystours (makers of saddle-trees), a reminder that throughout the Middle Ages, many artists, including the most renowned, were called upon to decorate saddles and harness. In Shrewsbury, where the glass-painters appear to have been few in number, it was with the saddlers that they combined to form a company. In Basle the glass-painters joined with the painters and saddlers.

By the end of the fifteenth century, the English glaziers' guilds were beginning to lose their pre-eminence, particularly in London. Barnard Flower's letter of appointment mentioned above is a most interesting document. Not only does it help to establish the nationality of this artist, hitherto thought to be German, but it also reveals that by the late fifteenth century, the King was no longer prepared to uphold the supremacy of the London Glaziers' Company against foreign competition. Flower was a resident of Southwark, describing himself in his will of 1517 as living in the 'precyntt of St Thomas the Martir Hospitall'. Galyon Hone, Flower's successor, resided in the ward of St Katherine, also beyond guild control. Earlier efforts to oppose the incursions of foreign competitors had enjoyed a measure of success, for in 1474 the London glaziers had successfully petitioned the mayor and aldermen against foreigners setting up businesses outside the city limits, while Richard III had forbidden the importation of windows painted abroad. When, in the 1540s, the London Guild petitioned Henry VIII against Hone and others who were neither freemen of the city nor members of the guild, men who 'refuse to be apprentyced saiyinge that they knowe an easyer way', one suspects that their pleas fell on deaf ears. Henry and his father both welcomed foreign artists to

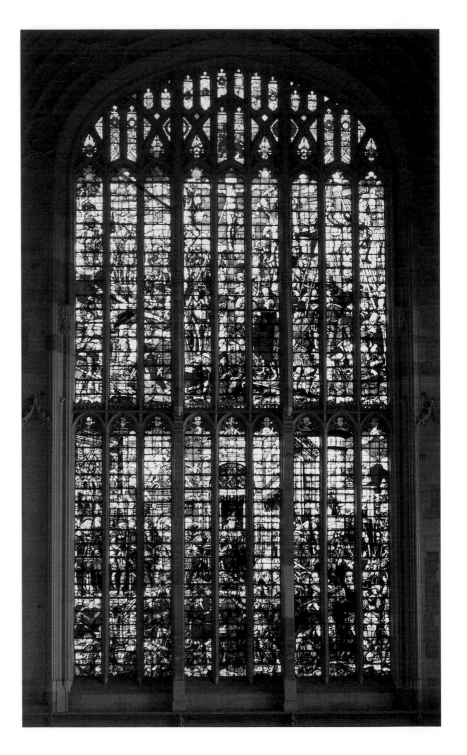

court and Bishop Foxe, entrusted with the general supervision of the glazing at King's College, where both Flower and Hone were to work, had travelled widely on the Continent where he had no doubt seen works in modern styles. Foxe was probably responsible for bringing Flower to the notice of Henry VII.

The fifteenth and early sixteenth centuries are also the period in which many more European glass-painters emerge from anonymity. Names can at last be matched to surviving windows – many of the outstanding windows in the church of St Lorenz in Nuremberg are known to have been glazed by the workshop of Michael Wolgemut, Albrecht Dürer's teacher, while in Angers Cathedral, the transept rose windows by André Robin, court painter to King Réné of Anjou, have survived. The careers of men such as Peter Hemmel, Arnold of Nijmegen and Jacob and Hans Acker, can be traced with some confidence. Peter Hemmel, who set up a workshop community with four independent masters during the 1470s, became so renowned that his Strasbourg workshop was called upon to supply

windows for Freiburg Cathedral, the church of Our Lady in Munich, St Lorenz in Nuremburg and Ulm Cathedral. Although Hemmel appears to have remained in Strasbourg, despatching finished windows to his many clients, there is also evidence in the late Middle Ages of much greater mobility in the profession, inevitably leading to the cross-fertilisation of one regional school with ideas and influences from another. Arnold of Nijmegen, for example, began his career in Tournai in Flanders, moved to Rouen in 1502, remaining there for twelve years and creating windows that bear his signature for the churches of St Godard and St Ouen. In 1513 he returned to Tournai, but remained in contact with his Rouen colleagues and pupils.

In the late fifteenth century, a number of foreign glass-painters were attracted to Spain – Nicolas Colin of Troyes is found working in Barcelona, while Thierry de Mes (possibly Metz) was employed at Saragossa. In the sixteenth century, two foreign artists, the Frenchman Guillaume de Marcillat and Konrad Much, a German called 'De Mochis', or 'Corrado da Colonia', by the Italians, made significant contributions to Italian stained glass. De Marcillat, born in 1467, was invited to Rome in 1506 by Pope Julius II, and worked at the Vatican alongside Bramante and Michaelangelo. Two windows in Santa Maria del Popolo survive from this period of his career. He later moved to Arezzo and made windows in San Francesco and Sta Anunziata and also painted frescoes in the Cathedral. While in Arezzo he came to the notice of the biographer Vasari who said of his work: 'these are not windows, but marvels, fallen from heaven for the consolation of men'. Konrad Much left his native Cologne in 1544 to head the glazing workshop of Milan Cathedral, where from 1568–70 he executed designs by Pelegrino Tibaldi whose cartoons survive in the Pinacoteca Ambrosiana. He was to be succeeded by another northern artist, the Fleming Valerius Diependale, from Louvain.

Throughout late medieval Europe, glass-painters were influenced by fellow artists working on panels and frescoes. In England, as we have seen, this contributed to the demise of the native guilds who could not match the inno-

24 *Opposite* The great east window of King's College Chapel, Cambridge, depicting the climax of the Passion sequence and, in the centre of the upper register, the Crucifixion itself. On 30 April 1526 Galyon Hone, the King's Glazier, together with Richard Bond, Thomas Reeve and James Nicholson, was commissioned to glaze the east and west windows and sixteen others in the Chapel.

25 *Right* St Ambrose, one of the four Latin Doctors of the Church, is depicted in this panel from the Konhofer window in the church of St Lorenz in Nuremberg. The window was donated *c.*1477 by Dr Konrad Konhofer, parish priest of St Lorenz, and was executed by the workshop of Michael Wolgemut, master of Albrecht Dürer.

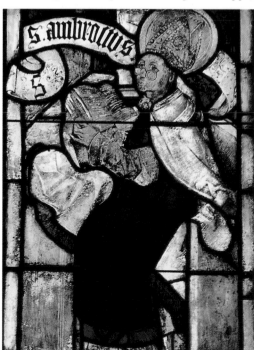

vative skills and modern styles of glass-painters conversant with the art of the Low Countries, but in Europe it appears to have led to greater exchange between glass-painters and artists in other media. The influence of Van Eyck can already be discerned in the famous Annunciation window given to Bourges Cathedral *c.*1448–50 by Jacques Coeur, while the influence of Rogier van der Weyden can be seen in the great Coronation of the Virgin window in the church of St Gommaire, at Lierre in Belgium. Bernard van Orley, author of the impressive Charles V window in Brussels Cathedral, travelled to Rome at the beginning of the sixteenth century where he worked with Raphael. On his return, he was appointed painter to the court, creating paintings, tapestries and increasingly, near the end of his life, stained glass, all of which were influential in spreading Italian styles north of the Alps.

The increasing proliferation of woodcuts and engravings in the years following the middle of the fifteenth century meant that the influence of a design could be felt far beyond the city of its origin. One of the artists whose work was most copied in this way was Albrecht Dürer, whose influence extended way beyond his native Nuremberg. His *Engraved Passion* published in 1512, for example, was known to the glass-painters responsible for the 1529 east window of Balliol College, Oxford, where it was the basis for the Agony in the Garden and the *Ecce Homo*. Romain Buron's debt to the German engraver Aldegrever was acknowledged by the letters alluding to his name painted on the hem of St Louis' garment in one of Buron's windows in the choir of Sainte Foy in Conches. Mobility and the easier transmission of artistic models in the sixteenth century confirmed stained glass as a truly international art form.

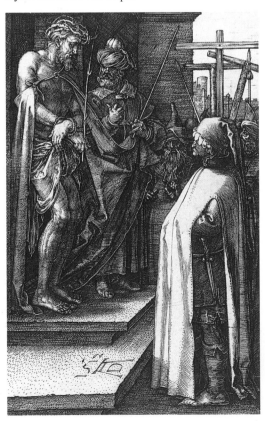

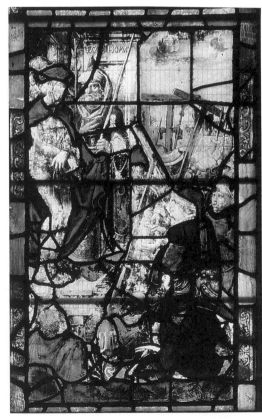

26, 27 Even in its poorly preserved state, it is possible to see that the design of the *Ecce Homo* panel of 1529 in the east window of Balliol College, Oxford (far right), is indebted to Dürer's immensely influential engraving of the subject published in 1512 (right), although the glass-painter has modified the scene and has added figures in the foreground.

4 THE PATRON AND THE GLASS-PAINTER

Apart from the two windows above the sedilia, each of the fourteen side windows of Merton College Chapel, Oxford, contains a single standing figure of an apostle, flanked by two figures of the same kneeling benefactor, identifiable from a series of inscriptions bearing the words *Henricus de Mamesfeld me fecit*, (Henry de Mamesfeld made me). Thus the donor could easily be mistaken for the artist, but a glass-painter Henry Mamesfeld certainly was not. He was a scholar and cleric, Chancellor of Oxford University and later Dean of Lincoln. The repetitive inscriptions and unavoidable image of the donor merely reflect the relative status of

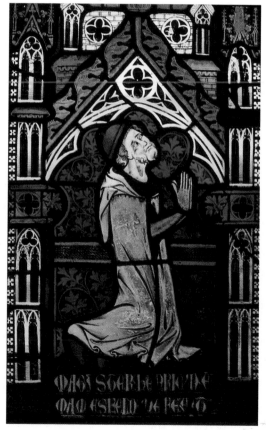

28 One of twenty-four 'portraits' of Henry de Mamesfield, the donor of the fourteen side windows in the choir of Merton College Chapel, Oxford. Mamesfield was Fellow of the College from 1288 until 1296 and was Chancellor of the University from 1309 to 1312. He left Oxford to become Dean of Lincoln and died in 1328.

patron and artist, for through much of the Middle Ages it was the patron, the man or woman who paid for the work of art and determined its form and content, who was regarded as its true creator. As has been stated before, the artist remained largely unacknowledged.

The interiors of most medieval churches were often enriched by the munificence of a relatively small number of wealthy men and women. In the feudal countryside, where a parish priest was often little more than the appointee of the lord of the manor, the church was filled with monuments, brasses, wall-paintings and windows paid for and often commemorating a few families. In the towns, the religious and secular guilds vied with individual wealthy merchants and craftsmen, the local nobility and secular churchmen, for the honour of beautifying the churches. The friary churches of the great preaching orders, the Dominicans and Franciscans, were particularly successful in attracting the patronage of the urban rich, although in cities like York, Chartres and Freiburg, the great cathedrals also attracted considerable patronage. One is struck by the diversity of medieval patrons both ecclesiastics and laypeople, who commissioned stained glass.

Many gifts to the church, including stained glass windows, were posthumous and wills provide a rich fund of information on devotional tastes and personal piety. The documentary records and the windows themselves suggest that they were given for a variety of reasons. Some were donated as simple acts of personal commemoration, as, for example, in the parish church of East Harling in Norfolk. There the east window was the gift of Anne Harling (*d*.1498), who outlived three husbands and asked to be buried next to her first, Sir William Chamberlain, in the chapel of St Anne in East Harling. The window depicted Anne with her first and second husbands and her father and mother. Anne also left vestments, a mass book, altar furnishings and the sum of 100s. to the church and her will also describes bequests to pay for her arms together with those of her first husband to be erected in glass in the churches of the Abbey of Wymondham, the White Friars in Cambridge, and the priories of Castle Acre and West Acre. Anne was the daughter of a famous and heroic soldier, heiress to a considerable fortune and was herself to die childless, the last representative of her line. The desire to leave a tangible and lasting trace of her passage through the world was a strong one and as the owner of nineteen manors, she was able to do it in style.

It is equally clear, however, that patronage of the Church was also regarded in part as a responsibility that attached itself to rank and social status. Certainly, its detractors attacked it for these reasons. John Wyclif, whose ideas were the basis for the Lollard movement in fifteenth-century England, had questioned on theological grounds the practice of revering religious imagery, and the ostentatious donations of stained glass windows are specifically singled out for condemnation in William Langland's late fourteenth-century *Vision of Piers Plowman*, in which the worldly Lady Mede is offered absolution for her sins in return for glazing a window.

It would be wrong, however, to underestimate the fundamentally spiritual motivation of most patrons of stained glass windows. This dimension is clearly manifest in the East Harling window which contained an inscription requesting prayers for the souls of the departed. The act of giving to the Church was in itself an act of spiritual benefit. In 1306, Archbishop Greenfield of York encouraged benefaction to the building fund of the new nave by offering an Indulgence, and in 1441 a Papal Indulgence was offered to those who donated alms for the conservation and repair of Holy Trinity, Tattershall.

Reconstructing the relationship between the patron and the artist in his employ is a difficult task. The reliance on private and individual acts of benefaction in the beautification of most churches and even the greatest cathedrals means that very few contracts and commissioning records survive. Most of the references to the glazing of York Minster, for example, deal not,

as one might expect, with the Minster's remarkable stained glass, but with plain glazing and mundane repairs. The majority of the windows were commissioned not by the Dean and Chapter but by individuals, clergy and laymen, and so contracts and documents remained in private hands with even less chance of survival than those in public and ecclesiastical archives. The only two contracts to survive for York do so because they were copied into Minster records and related to the gift of an Archbishop 29 – Melton's gift of the west windows, and the Dean and Chapter's own employment of Thornton to undertake the east window. A valuable exception to this paucity of documentary evidence, in England at least, is to be found in royal records. England's kings were generous patrons of glass-painters: Henry III was particularly committed to architectural and artistic projects and stained glass is mentioned many times in his household accounts.

There can be no doubt that the tastes of the patron could profoundly affect the nature of the glazing scheme. The remarkably homogeneous glazing of the east end of Canterbury Cathedral, firmly directed by the wealthy monastic community of Christ Church, with its careful division into windows for monastic contemplation and public edification, can be compared to the

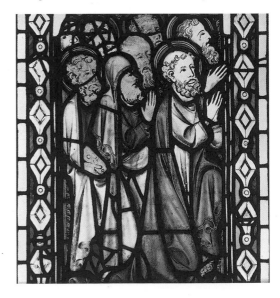

29 On 4 February 1339 Archbishop William Melton of York gave 100 marks for the glazing of the west window of the Minster. Seventeenth-century copies of the glazing contracts preserve the names of two glass-painters, Master Robert employed to glaze the west window (seen here), and Thomas Bouesdon, employed to glaze the side aisle windows.

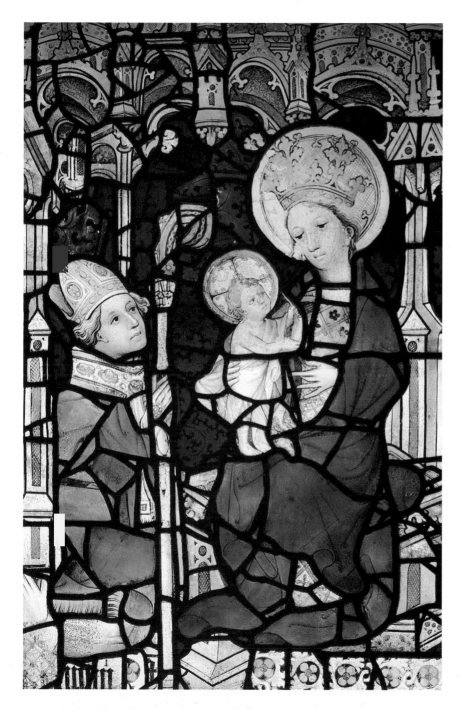

iconographic inconsistencies of the glazing scheme of Chartres, with no fewer than five windows dedicated to St James the Great, paid for by a variety of donors. Such comparison demonstrates very clearly the effect of patronage factors.

Windows often contain clear visual evidence of the personal devotional preferences of the donors. Most commonly, this gave rise to the depiction of the donor's name-saint – Cardinal Thomas Wolsey is identified with St Thomas Becket, Queen Margaret of Scotland is accompanied by Saint Margaret in the Chapel of the Vyne in Hampshire, and in the nave of York Minster a layman identified only as 'Vincent' kneels below a depiction of the martyrdom of his namesake. Particular devotions of a less obvious nature emerge when the patrons have been responsible for a number of pious benefactions. Bishop William of Wykeham's special devotion was reserved for the Virgin Mary at whose feet he kneels in Winchester College Chapel. Thomas Spofford, Bishop of Hereford, had a demonstrable devotion to St Anne – he kneels at her feet in a very restored image in the east window of the church of St Lawrence in Ludlow, and in glass from the Hereford episcopal palace of Stretton Sugwas, now in Ross-on-Wye, he offers her his heart. The appearance of the unusual Exeter saint, Sidwell, in the chapel windows of All Souls College, Oxford, reflects the initiative of Roger Keyes, supervisor of the college buildings. From 1436 he was a canon of Exeter Cathedral and had been instrumental in resolving a dispute involving the manor of 'St Sydwelles without Eastgate' in the Dean and Chapter's favour.

One perhaps surprising fact emerges from the few surviving English documents and glazing contracts, namely that the proposed subject matter and physical appearance of the window

30 William of Wykeham's devotion to the Virgin, at whose feet he kneels in this panel in Winchester College Chapel, was expressed in the dedications of his two great colleges, both dedicated to her: New College, Oxford, founded in 1379, and 'Seinte Marie College of Wynchestre', founded in 1382. The chapels of both were furnished with fine stained glass by the workshop of Thomas Glazier of Oxford.

is rarely mentioned. The contracts of 1338/9 relating to the west windows of York Minster make no mention at all of the contents of the windows. Nor do the Exeter records mention subject matter. The 'subjects and figures' to be drawn by John Thornton are not described in his contract of 1405 and in the 1482 glazing accounts for Holy Trinity Church, Tattershall, Lincolnshire, the mention of the principal subjects of the windows, the Legend of the Holy Cross, St James, the Creed, the Magnificat, and the Seven Sacraments, appears to be designed as much to differentiate between the different glazing teams led by Robert Power, John Glazier, John Wymondswalde, Thomas Woodshawe and Richard Twygge, as to convey an accurate impression of what the windows were to look like. The agreement with the glaziers Galyon Hone, Richard Bond, Thomas Reve and James Nicholson, for eighteen windows in King's College, Cambridge, states merely that the subject is to be 'the olde lawe and of newe lawe after the fourme maner goodenes curyousytie and clenelynes in euery poynt of the glasse wyndowes of the kynges new Chapell at Westmynster'.

It can only be concluded that the contract was a formal recognition that a commission had been extended by a patron and accepted by a painter, and defined the financial responsibilities of both parties. The exact details of content and decorative repertoire must have been discussed and settled at an earlier stage and could be more easily expressed as a picture than in words. It was presumably the sketch design, the *vidimus*, that client and artist regarded as the record of what the window was to look like. Very few of these sketches have survived. Of those that do, most are late in date, although it has been frequently suggested that the Guthlac Roll of about 1200, may in some way be related to a series of medallion designs for stained glass.

Evidence for the *vidimus* is more plentiful at the close of the Middle Ages. In the National Gallery of Scotland an annotated sketch of about 1520–30, attributed to Erhard Schön, an artist close to Dürer, but with notes that may be in the hand of the English glazier James Nicholson, depicts a huge thirteen-light window with scenes above and below a transom. The presence in the lower register of St William of York and St Thomas of Canterbury suggests that the

32, conte
page

31 *Left* Only four from an original seven scenes of the Corporal Acts of Mercy survive in Holy Trinity Church, Tattershall, Lincolnshire, but they can with confidence be attributed to the workshop of Richard Twygge and Thomas Woodshawe, who were also responsible for the Seven Sacraments window. Twygge was later employed in 1507–8 to glaze fourteen clerestory windows at Westminster Abbey.

32 *Right* The window for which this design in the National Gallery of Scotland was prepared has either not survived or was never executed. It has been attributed to Hampton Court Chapel, but may have been intended for the unbuilt chapel of Cardinal Wolsey's great unrealised educational enterprise, Cardinal College in Oxford.

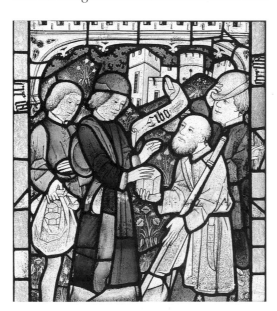

design was commissioned for an English prelate, very plausibly for Thomas Wolsey, Archbishop of York, papal legate and a great builder and patron of stained glass. A further twenty-four drawings of windows in the print room of the Musées Royaux des Beaux Arts in Brussels have also been attributed to Wolsey's patronage and were perhaps destined for the chapel of Hampton Court Palace. They depict a cycle of the Life and Passion of Christ, the apostles and saints, prophets and doctors of the Church, together with donor figures of a king and queen and a cardinal.

Two notable English verbal equivalents to the *vidimus* deserve mention. One relates to a royal commission and is found in two rolls now preserved in the British Library in London, containing detailed instructions for the glazing of the Church of the Observant or Reformed Friars in Greenwich. The church was built in the reign of Henry VII and was completed in 1493–4. A single large window, probably intended for either the east or west end, was to include figures of Louis of France, Ethelbert and Edith. The instructions for St Etheldreda are typical: 'Seint Audry, a Kynges doughter shryned at Ely, make her in thabytte of a nonne wyth an opyn crowne crowned, wyth a croyse in her ryghte honde, a booke in the left honde, a mantill of her armes'. Each figure was to be accompanied by a shield of arms, and these were painted in the margins rather than described. Quite why the glass-painters were instructed in this way is difficult to discern although it is possible that here, as in other commissions of Henry VII's reign, foreign glass-painters were employed, perhaps unfamiliar with the typical attributes of English saints like Etheldreda and Ethelbert. That the coats of arms were depicted visually rather than verbally may point to the glass-painters' unfamiliarity with the terms of heraldic blazon, although, as we shall see, there is also evidence that patrons lacked confidence in their artists in this quarter.

The second example relates to a more humble commission, which unlike the Greenwich window, partially remains. In his will dated 5 April 1500, Henry Williams, vicar of Stanford on Avon in Northamptonshire from 1486 until 1501, specified: 'I wyll that the glasses windowes in the chancell wth ymagery that was thereyn before allso wth my ymage knelying in ytt and the ymage of deth shotyng at me, another wyndowe before Saynt John with ymagery in ytt now wth my ymage knelyng in ytt and deth shoting at me thys be done in smalle quarells of as gude glasse as can be goten'. Henry's executors observed his wishes and a single tiny kneeling figure faces a roundel with a skeleton firing an arrow from a bow.

In some instances, it is clear that not only did the patron select a subject for a window, he also provided the model from which the glass-painters worked. The Becket miracle windows in the ambulatory of the Trinity Chapel of Canterbury Cathedral contain a series of scenes which depict miraculous events that took place at Becket's tomb between 1171 and 1173, which were described in two prose lives of St Thomas written by two Canterbury monks, Benedict and William. The panels contain complicated Latin inscriptions that required translation by the monks who accompanied the visiting pilgrims as they made their way to the shrine. In some cases, the panel depicts an amalgamated version of a miraculous incident culled from the two sources. It seems unlikely that this iconographic scheme, reliant on such precise literary sources,

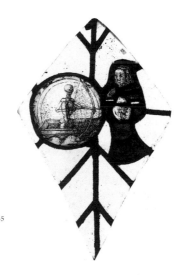

33 This extract from a roll of instructions for the glazing of the Church of the Observant Friars in Greenwich describes the figures of Saint Louis of France, King Ethelbert of Kent (illustrated here) and Saint Edith. The written descriptions are augmented by sketches to show the correct appearance of the coats of arms which were to accompany each figure.

34 This unprepossessing panel in the church of St Nicholas, Stanford on Avon, is all that survives of Henry Williams' 'small quarells of as gude glasse as can be goten'. Although the evidence for glazing in medieval wills is plentiful, it is extremely rare for both the document and the stained glass to have survived.

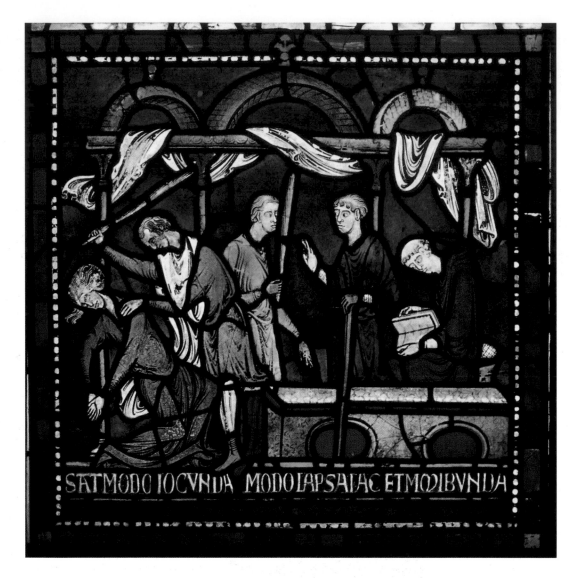

35 This lively scene from the Trinity Chapel of Canterbury Cathedral shows an episode in the cure of Mathilda, a madwoman of Cologne. She is shown in a swoon before the crypt tomb of St Thomas Becket, the destination of pilgrims before the construction of the shrine in the choir to which St Thomas was translated in 1220.

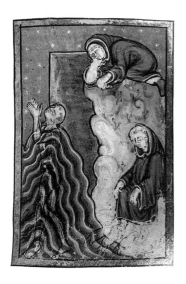

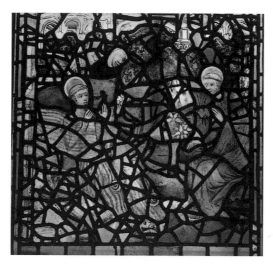

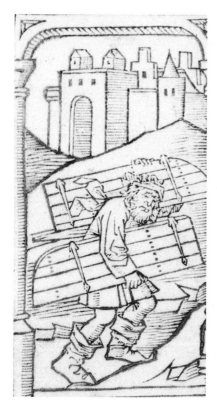

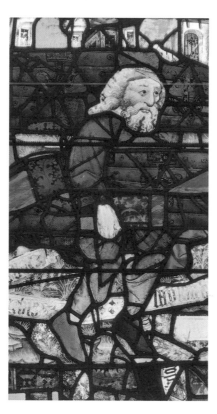

was the creation of a glazing workshop. Certainly, the Latin inscriptions at very least would have required the supervision of the Christ Church monks. The St Cuthbert window in York Minster, the gift of Bishop Langley of Durham, has now been shown to be indebted for much of its iconography to an early twelfth-century manuscript of Bede's *Life of St Cuthbert*, in the possession of Durham Cathedral Priory. It was presumably the patron who brought this extensive narrative of Cuthbert's life to the attention of the glass-painters.

A more up-to-date model was used for the choir glazing of 1466–80 at the church of the Holy Trinity, Tattershall, Lincolnshire. The source for the selection of Old and New Testament types and antitypes has been shown to be the forty-page block book edition of the *Biblia Pauperum*, first produced in the Netherlands in about 1464–5. Familiarity with it at Tattershall so soon after its Continental publication may be a reflection of the reading habits of the high-status donors rather than the literary sophistication of the glass-painters.

Finally, the iconography of the Last Supper in the east window of Great Malvern priory, sometimes attributed to John Thornton's workshop and dating from *c*.1420–30, may also owe something to a manuscript model. The panel shows Judas Iscariot stealing a fish from the

36, 37 *Top* Although three hundred years separate these two scenes of St Cuthbert praying in the sea, it is clear that the early twelfth-century manuscript *Life of St Cuthbert* (left), made for Durham Cathedral Priory, served as the source for the fifteenth-century St Cuthbert window in York Minster (right), the gift of Bishop Langley of Durham. Although damage to the panel of glass has reduced its clarity, the relationship between the two can still be discerned.

38, 39 *Left* The *Biblia Pauperum* was an immensely popular text throughout the Middle Ages. That the influence of the forty-page block-book edition (left) quickly made itself felt in England can be seen in the stained glass depiction (right) of Samson and the Gates of Gaza from Holy Trinity, Tattershall (now in St Martin's Church, Stamford), which relies heavily upon the block-book model.

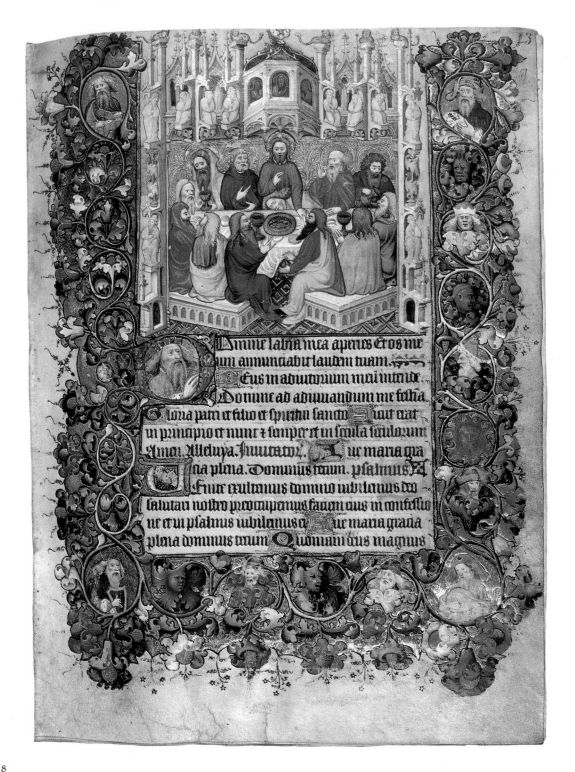

40, 41 Although the exact nature of the relationship between this manuscript (left) and a panel of stained glass in the east window of Great Malvern Priory (opposite) cannot be determined, the shared motif of Judas hiding the fish, an unusual incident in the depiction of the Last Supper, may reflect the influence of a common patron.

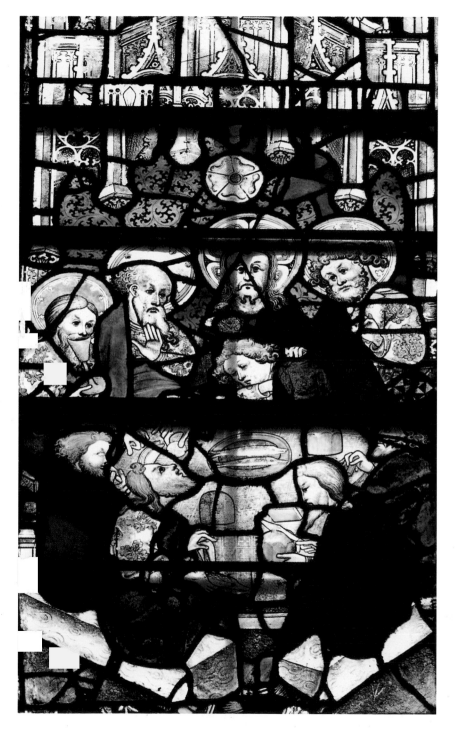

table, a detail also found in the roughly contemporary manuscript known, because of a later owner, as the *Hours of Elizabeth the Queen.* [40] Although it is not known for whom the book was first made, it had belonged early in its life to Cecily, wife of Henry Beauchamp, Duke of Warwick between 1445 and 1446. The Malvern window was possibly the gift of Richard Beauchamp, Henry's predecessor. If the manuscript was in Beauchamp hands from its creation, it may well have provided ideas for the glass-painters at Great Malvern.

While Bishop Langley must have specified that the Bede *Life of St Cuthbert* manuscript was to provide the model for the St Cuthbert window in York, the glass-painters are unlikely to have been allowed direct access to such a treasure, and the nature of the intermediary drawings used to prepare the full-scale outlines on the whitewashed trestles is impossible to decide. There is certainly evidence that donors sometimes employed artists not normally involved in stained glass in the preparation of sketches to be translated into glass. At the Beauchamp Chapel, John Prudde was apparently faced with something of a design *fait accompli*, receiving from the Executors 'patterns of paper, afterwards to be newly traced and pictured by another painter at the charge of the said Glasier'. As these drawings required translation into a form from which the glaziers could work, presumably a scaled transfer to the whitewashed trestles, it can be assumed that they were not full-scale cartoons, which would, of course, need no translation. Perhaps it was patterns of this kind that Bishop Langley provided for the glass-painters in York.

The evidence of the Greenwich instructions illustrated with heraldic sketches, suggests that donors were particularly unwilling to leave glass-painters to their own devices where heraldry was concerned. And not without good reason, it would seem, from Lady Margaret Beaufort's experience at Collyweston: in 1505, John Delyon of Peterborough was employed to glaze the manor house there, and mistakenly depicted the heraldic yale as a common antelope. He was paid 7s. 'for the changying of the Antelope unto an Ivell [yale] in the bay wyndow in the grett chambre, wt xxd yeveyn [given] to William Hollmer for the draght of the said Ivell at London'. It had apparently been necessary to provide Delyon with a working drawing supplied by an artist more expert in heraldic work.

Continental evidence that patrons sometimes provided glass-painters with cartoons commissioned from painters is relatively plentiful, particularly from the late Middle Ages. Probably the most famous artist thus employed was Dürer, who drew cartoons for the Schmidtmayer Chapel in the church of St Lorenz in Nuremberg. His pupils, Hans von Kulmbach and Hans Baldung Grien also executed cartoons for glass: Kulmbach cartooned glass executed by Veit Hirsvogel in St Sebald's in Nuremberg; and Grien, who worked extensively in glass, cartooned, for example, the weeping woman from 42, 24 the choir of Freiburg Cathedral, executed by Hans Gitschmann von Ropstein, and now in the Augustiner Museum there. That the evidence for these commissions is late is hardly surprising; the availability of affordable paper in the late medieval period undermined reliance on the unwieldy whitewashed table, and made it more feasible for full-scale cartoons to be prepared outside the glass-painter's workshop.

The relatively early date at which paper was available to Italian artists no doubt explains the apparently common practice of commissioning cartoons from painters and sculptors rather than directly from the glass-painters. Paper is mentioned in connection with the glazing of Siena Cathedral as early as 1355. Cennino Cennini's *Libro dell' Arte* of the late fourteenth century suggests that by that date the designs and cartoons for windows were rarely carried out in the glazier's workshop. Thus, in the 1350s, Simone Martini provided cartoons for the windows of the lower church in Assisi as well as executing the mural decoration. In the 1440s Taddeo Gaddi worked on the frescoes of the Baroncelli Chapel in Sta Croce in Florence and also provided cartoons for the window. In fifteenth-century Florence the city commissioned cartoons for the windows of the Duomo from the leading painters and sculptors of the day. Lorenzo Ghiberti, best known for the Baptistry doors, designed the occuli of the west

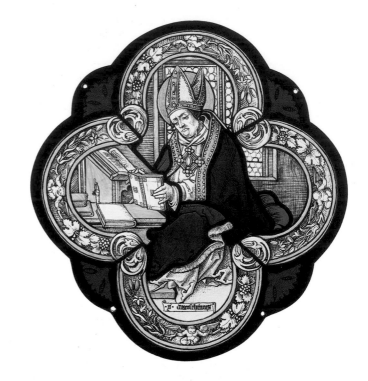

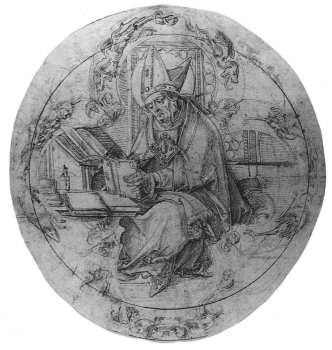

42, 43 *Opposite* In the
execution of this panel
depicting St Augustine of
Hippo in his study in *c.*1507
(top), the stained glass artist
has adapted a design (bottom)
suitable for either a medallion
or quatrefoil treatment and he
uses a simplified border
design. The glass, painted by
the workshop of Veit
Hirsvogel the Elder, is from an
unidentified Nuremberg
church, while the cartoon is
attributed to Dürer's pupil
Hans Suess Kulmbach.

facade. The eleven circular windows, or *occhi*, of the cupola were also glazed. Paolo Uccello was entrusted with the Resurrection, the Nativity and a third which has been lost, and Andrea del Castagno with the Descent from the Cross. Less successful was Donatello's Coronation of the Virgin, commissioned in place of a rejected Ghiberti design. Ghiberti contributed a further three windows to the cupola: the Ascension (1444), the Garden of Gethsemane (1444) and Presentation in the Temple (1445).

When writing about fifteenth-century Italian painting, Michael Baxandall reminded his readers that 'money is very important in the History of Art'. This observation could just as easily be applied to the history of glass-painting, cost being the overwhelming concern of the very few glazing accounts or contracts that do survive. The way in which the donors chose to spend their money had a profound affect on the appearance of the window. They were faced with a number of choices. Most windows were paid for by the square foot, as completed panels. Within the price agreed for the finished article, a number of determinant factors came into play. These can be divided broadly into two kinds of cost — those of materials and those of technical and artistic skill. The 1447 contract for the glazing of the Beauchamp Chapel, a commission of particular sumptuousness, specified that only the very best materials, imported from overseas, were to be used, with the range of colours to be employed carefully stipulated:

> the said John Prudde doeth covenant to glasse all these windowes in the new Chapel in Warwick with glasse of beyound the seas, and with noe glasse of England, and that in the finest wise with the best, cleanest, and strongest glasse of beyonde the seas that may be had in England, and of the finest colours of blew, yellow, red, purpure, sanguine, and violet, and all other colours that shall be most necessary and best.

It is clear that the more complicated and richly coloured the window, the higher the cost involved. J. A. Knowles constructed a price list for the various types of work undertaken by John Prudde. The cheapest panels at 7d. per foot, were of plain white glass for Shene Palace; quarry windows with figures of prophets ('powdred glasse cum xij ymaginibus prophetarum')

for Eton College Chapel at 8d. per foot; in 1445–6 figures with borders for Eton cost 1s. per foot; in 1449–50 *vitri historialis*, presumably narrative windows, for Eton College Hall cost 1s. 2d. per foot; and at the top of the scale the Beauchamp Chapel windows, with their expensive foreign glasses and rich jewelled borders, cost 2s. per foot in 1447. This was not, however, the most costly glazing recorded, for in 1402 Henry IV paid William Burgh 3s. 4d. per foot for windows 'diapered and worked with broom flowers, eagles, and scrolls inscribed *Souveraigne*' for Eltham Palace. These panels were for the King's private appartments and must have been splendid indeed.

In contrast, the contract of 1405 between the Dean and Chapter of York and John Thornton of Coventry laid emphasis on the painting skills of the master. Having specified the wages that he was to receive, the Dean and Chapter went on to state that not only was Thornton 'to draw the window and the subjects, figures and any other things to be painted on the same' but he was himself 'to paint the same where need required according to the ordination of the Dean and Chapter'. Numerous hands of varying degrees of skill and refinement can be detected in the east window of York Minster, but the superb quality of heads such as that of St Edward the Confessor suggests that Thornton did indeed observe the Dean and Chapter's stipulations and reserved some of the most important figures for his own hand.

Although purchase of completed panels by the square foot was the norm, in exceptional circumstances, the patron could also bring about the creation for a short period of time of special workshops to execute special commissions. St Stephen's Chapel, Westminster, is one such example. The roll of accounts of Robert de Campsale, Clerk of Works for the royal palace of Westminster, reveals that as early as July 1349 coloured glass, materials and tools were being purchased, and in the following year quantities of canvas to serve as temporary fillings for the completed window openings. In March 1350 John de Lincoln was appointed master glazier and was authorised to select a work-force from all over England. Further purchases of glass

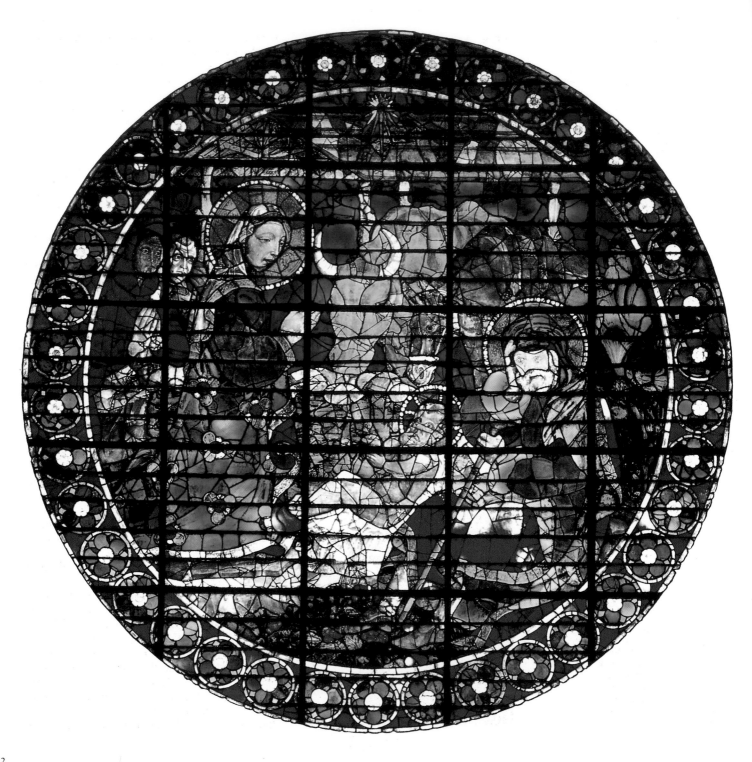

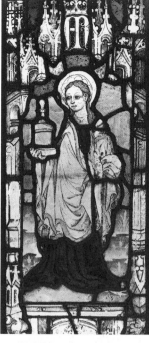

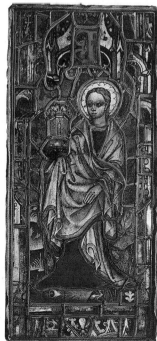

44 *Opposite* The Nativity, drawn in 1443, was one of the three scenes commissioned for the *occhi* of Florence Cathedral from the artist Paolo Uccello. The Resurrection also survives, although the third window executed to an Uccello design, the Annunciation, was lost in the nineteenth century.

45, 46 *Right* Although distinguishable by their initials and their different attributes, it is clear that St Mary Magdalen (above) and St Barbara (below, and here photographed from the back to make comparison easier) from an unidentified Norfolk location, originated on the same glazier's whitewashed table.

were also authorised. Detailed accounts survive for the period 20 June 1351 to March 1352. A total of £240 was spent on the glazing, by far the largest sum being £195, the total of the glass-painters' wages.

In 1399 preparations were already in hand for the glazing of the east window of York Minster. The Dean and Chapter set about equipping a glazing workshop for this commission. White and coloured glass was purchased, a kiln constructed and soldering irons, clamps and tongs bought. Only on 10 December 1405 was a contract of employment with a master glazier finally signed, awarding John Thornton £46 in wages and gratuities, with a £10 bonus if the work was completed within the three-year period stipulated. Thornton was also authorised to take on additional staff. By 1410, with the east window complete, he established himself as an independent master and freeman of the city. Although no other work is documented, his workshop executed many other windows for the Minster, no doubt paid for by the foot by clients other than the Dean and Chapter.

Does all this evidence of the powerful influence of the patron mean that glass-painters made no creative contribution to the execution of a glazing commission? The evidence above relates to exceptional commissions, with exceptional patrons. The high proportion of simple, not to say formulaic windows in humble parish churches suggests that many patrons had conventional tastes and were guided in their choices by their own limited experience of religious art or by the professional advice of glass-painters inclined to favour pragmatic adaptation over creative originality. The use through much of the medieval period of a whitewashed table encouraged the reuse and the sensible adaptation of a composition where possible, most frequently by reversing it or adding different attributes or accessories to the same basic figure, as, for example, in the case of two female saints 45, 46 from the same unidentified Norfolk location, now divided between the Burrell Collection in Glasgow and the Metropolitan Museum in New York. And yet the unwieldy nature of the table, usually cleaned and redrawn between commissions, also ensured that these adaptations are

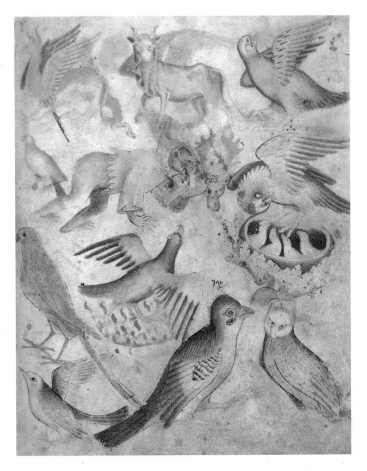

the result of a glass-painter with an undemanding client producing two panels for the price of one design, or had a visiting client seen and admired the composition in the workshop and specifically requested a more or less identical panel? Until the widespread adoption of paper cartoons in the late Middle Ages, it was not easy or indeed practical to preserve full-scale designs and variations in window size meant that there was little point anyway.

What seems far more plausible is that less educated, or simply less self-assured patrons would seek the guidance of the master glass-painter, and perhaps his parish priest, in the selection of a design for a window and could peruse the medieval equivalent of a workshop catalogue. There is increasing evidence that artists in all media kept sketch-books and pattern-books to serve as a guide to both workshop members and clients. It has been suggested that the Pepysian sketch-book at Magdalene College, Cambridge, served such a purpose in a glass-painter's workshop − the beautifully depicted birds could have served as models for the bird quarries like those found at Clothall, Hertfordshire, and Buckland Rectory, Gloucestershire. The wills of the York glass-painters Thomas Shirley (*d.*1456) and William English (*d.*1480) both refer to workshop drawings (*protractoria* and *picturis opelle*), and the fact that the drawings of the Pepysian sketch-book are of a variety of dates, the earliest around 1370−90 and the latest late fifteenth century or early sixteenth century, suggests that it was in use in a workshop over quite a period of time, with successive generations of artists adding to it.

The evidence of Theophilus, a reliable and accurate source in so many other things, cannot be lightly discarded. In instructing the glass-painter as to the use of the whitewashed table, he says: 'take the dimensions − length and breadth − of one section of the window, and, using a rule and compass, mark them on the board with lead or tin. If you want to have a border on it, mark out the width you want and the workmanship that you desire. This done, draw whatever figures you have chosen'. It is certainly true that Cennino's evidence denies the glass-painter a role as designer, but as we

47 The drawings of figures, animals and birds, mostly dating from *c.*1370−90, could have served as models for artists of most media. The appearance of a window tracery design on folio 17 verso has prompted the suggestion that it was in use in a glazier's workshop. The addition of sketches in the late fifteenth or early sixteenth century, reveals that the book had a long working life.

almost always confined to a single window or series of windows within one building within a short time span. The thirteenth-century apostles in the north transept of Chartres Cathedral are drawn from one cartoon, as are many of the early fourteenth-century figures in the choir clerestory of the parish church of St Pierre in Chartres. St Peter in prison in the fifteenth-century Bowet window in the north choir aisle of York Minster becomes St John the Baptist in prison in the south aisle of the choir. More interesting and harder to explain is the use of an identical cartoon for two fourteenth-century depictions of the Virgin and Child in the parish churches of Fladbury and Warndon, both in Worcestershire, and only ten miles apart. Is this

have seen the status of the craft was rather different in Italy from that north of the Alps.

There is also documentary evidence to support the role of the glass-painter as a designer. The value of design was recognised in financial terms at St Stephen's Chapel, Westminster. From late June to late July 1351, John de Chester was paid a steady 7s. per week, irrespective of saints' days and holidays, to produce designs for the other glass-painters. On 3 October 1351, six masters received 1s. per day each for six days for 'designing and painting on white tables'.

The few surviving *vidimi* also suggest that the glass-painter acted as creative adviser to his patron. The Edinburgh drawing is annotated with notes suggesting alternative arrangements of figures. The Brussels drawings offer further evidence of the refining of the design: two versions of the Crucifixion are offered, one with sorrowing angels and one without. The other drawings are profusely annotated, with erasures and changes of mind.

The visual testimony of the east window of York Minster also lends weight to the concept of the master glass-painter as designer. The east window with its complex and extensive narrative of the Apocalypse, contains scenes for which there is no direct model. The imaginative and harmonious solution of compositional problems suggests the hand of a master at ease with his medium and confirms Thornton as a designer of considerable talent as well as a painter of stature.

Successful medieval glass-painters were those able to satisfy a varied and demanding clientele. They were judged not only on their merits as artists, but on their skills as craftsmen and on their ability to give value for money. Their success in the diplomatic art of pleasing the customer can only be admired.

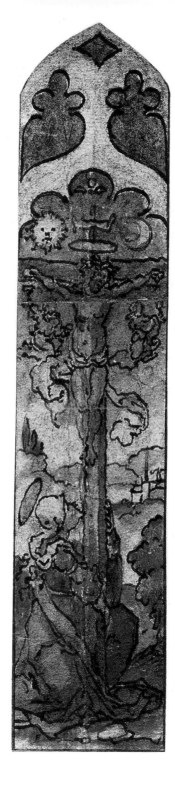
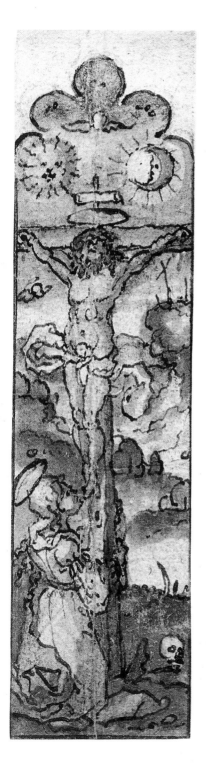

48, 49 The designer of the Crucifixion in these two sketches, preserved in the Musées Royaux in Brussels, was clearly unsure as to the doctrinal stance of his patron, probably Cardinal Thomas Wolsey. While both depict Mary Magdalen at the foot of the Cross, one (left) caters to the doctrine of the Real Presence by showing angels with chalices collecting the blood flowing from Christ's hands and side, while the other omits these angelic embellishments.

5 MAKING THE WINDOW

'For the human eye is not able to consider on what work first to fix its gaze; . . . if it regards the profusion of light from the windows, it marvels at the inestimable beauty of the glass and the infinitely rich and various workmanship.' (Theophilus, *The Various Arts*, Preface to Book III). This quotation makes it clear that because of its aesthetic contribution and the high levels of craftsmanship it demanded, stained glass was highly regarded in the Middle Ages. An appreciation of the skills shown by medieval glass-painters depends on some knowledge of the working methods and techniques which they used. Although the medium developed during the Middle Ages, it has remained remarkably consistent since then and one can learn much about medieval working methods by visiting one of the more traditional studios practising today.

Besides the evidence of the glass itself, and documentary sources like inventories and accounts, a small number of artists' treatises, mainly from Italy, give invaluable information on how medieval windows were made: they include a late fourteenth-century treatise by the Florentine stained glass artist Antonio da Pisa, the *Libro dell' Arte* of Cennino Cennini, and part of a treatise on technique by the famous Florentine artist and biographer Giorgio Vasari. By far the most important of these is Theophilus' *De Diversis Artibus*, 'The Various Arts', written in north-west Germany between about 1110 and 1140. Theophilus was the pseudonym of a Benedictine monk, who was possibly the metalworker Roger of Helmershausen. He was both a scholar writing about the artist from a theological point of view, and also a practising craftsman with a detailed technical knowledge of wall-painting, panel-painting, manuscript illumination, metalwork and ivory carving, as well as painted glass. The second of the three books which form the treatise is devoted to glass in its widest sense, with instructions on how to make plain and coloured glass, vessels and, in sections XVII to XXIX, stained glass windows. Theophilus was writing in the twelfth century and surviving glass of that date confirms the procedures that he describes, but as techniques remained fairly static his writings serve as a general guide to practice throughout the Middle Ages.

Although he begins by describing a kiln for making glass, it needs to be stressed that medieval glaziers and glass-painters hardly ever made their own glass; like today's practitioners they bought ready-made sheets, often from a merchant or other middleman, rather than directly from the glass-house. In an early scheme like the seventh-century glazing of Jarrow and Monkwearmouth, both in Northumberland, the craftsmen who made the glass may also have designed and executed the windows themselves, but in general this conflation of glass-maker and glazier was impractical and the two operations remained distinct. The medieval glass-painter was therefore dependent on others for a ready supply of raw materials and presumably had even more problems than today's artists in obtaining the right quantity, quality and colour of glass required.

Evidence is lacking for a detailed history of medieval glass-making but by the time Theophilus was writing, production seems to have been widespread in Europe, and flourished especially in those areas which were well established in Roman times. In the south this meant the coastal sites around the Mediterranean and probably included the island of Murano in the Venetian lagoon where glass-painters are recorded by the late thirteenth century. North of the Alps, glass-houses were concentrated in the forest areas where there were good supplies of the basic constituents of glass – sand (silica) and beech-wood (potash), which reduced the melting point of sand to give a material which was easier to work. The forests, of course, also provided the wood to fire the kilns. Bohemian glass-houses were in production by the four-

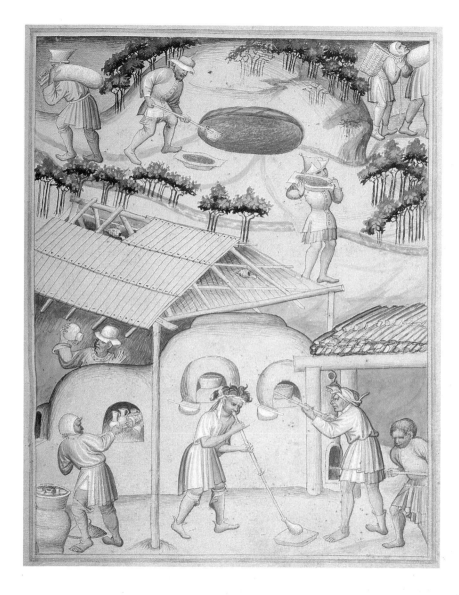

⁵⁰

50 A manuscript illumination of the Pit of Memnon from *The Travels of Sir John Mandeville* produced in Bohemia during the early fifteenth century. It provides a rare illustration of a medieval glass-house in operation.

teenth century and an early fifteenth-century illumination in a manuscript of Mandeville's *Travels* produced in this area shows a late medieval glass-house in operation with sandpit, 50 trees, blowpipe and kilns. Glass vessels are being made but such a glass-house could easily have produced window glass as well. Other northern areas of production included the Low Countries, the Rhineland area of Germany, Burgundy and Lorraine, and France, notably Normandy and the valleys of the Seine and Loire.

In late medieval England two main areas of glass-making stand out — in the south, the Weald area of Kent, Surrey and Sussex, and the Midland counties of Shropshire and Staffordshire. For the royal works at Westminster and Windsor in the middle of the fourteenth century John Alemayne and William Holmer provided white glass from Chiddingfold, one of the principal Weald sites, as did various Shropshire and Staffordshire glass-houses. In 1418 the Dean and Chapter of York purchased white glass from John Glasman of Rugeley, Staffordshire, and in 1478 were supplied by Edmund Bardale of Bramley buttes (Abbots Bromley) in the same county.

From the thirteenth century on, when glazing accounts become more common, there is little positive evidence for the manufacture of coloured window glass in England. It was presumably for this reason, and because of worries about the quality of native production, that the executors responsible for the Beauchamp Chapel, Warwick, were insistent that only foreign glass be used. Henry VI tried to get round this problem in 1449 by employing the Fleming, John Utynam, to make glass for the royal foundations at Eton and King's College, Cambridge, granting him a twenty-year monopoly on the manufacture of coloured window glass 'because the said art has never been used in England'. The evidence of late medieval documents proves that English glass-painters imported both white and coloured glass from the Continent. In 1317, for example, 629 pieces (sheets) of white glass were bought in Rouen at a cost of £15 14s. 9d. for glazing use at Exeter Cathedral. The Minster fabric rolls and the wills of glaziers in York show that late medieval craftsmen there bought sheets from English glass-houses *(vitri anglicani)* and from two major Continental sources, the Rhineland area of Burgundy, Hesse and Lorraine *(vitri Borgondie, Hass glas* and *Rennyshe)*, as well as from the Rouen area *(Normandie glas)*. For work at Coldharbor, London, in 1485. Herman Glasyer supplied window glass from England, Germany and Venice, and in 1497, once again in the capital, glass from Normandy and Venice was used for the glazing of the Pewterers' Hall.

In general the documents suggest that English glaziers and their patrons paid twice as much for coloured glass as for white glass, but in the accounts for St Stephen's Chapel, Westminster, white glass from Chiddingfold cost 6d. a wey, red glass cost 2s. 2d. and blue as much as 3s., that is six times the cost of white. Various terms are used in the documents to record the quantity of glass purchased, and this is usually estimated by weight. The wey or wisp weighed 5 lb (*c.*22.5 kg) and was sufficient for about 2 ft (*c.*60 cm) of glazing. The seam, another unit of glass, (later accounts refer to cases, chests or cradles) consisted of 24 weys, in other words, 120 lb (*c.*544 kg) in weight.

Two types of window glass were available to the medieval glazier. More common was that produced by the muff or cylinder process, in which the molten glass was blown into the form of a cylinder which was then cut along its length, reheated and flattened into a regular sheet with characteristic raised edges. The alternative method was the spun or crown process in which the glass was transferred from the blowpipe to a pontil iron which was spun round rapidly to produce a circular sheet by centrifugal force. Such sheets have a characteristic bull's eye at the centre and become thinner at the edge, with curving lines often preserved within the texture of the glass. Theophilus describes the making of a form of cylinder glass, but small sheets of crown glass are known from the Near East in the fourth century and they are used quite frequently in English and French windows of the first half of the fourteenth century. Glaziers working at neighbouring Beverley Minster and York Minster around 1340 deliberately chose thick bull's eyes to give a three-dimensional sculptural quality to some of their figures. In the Middle Ages glass was too valuable a commodity to be thrown away and thick bull's eyes which were difficult to lead into church windows could no doubt be used in domestic settings. Jost Amman's sixteenth-

51 Detail from a Swiss domestic panel of *c.*1580–90 from Kreuzenstein Castle in Austria. It shows the interior of a glazier's workshop where bull's eye windows are being leaded up and soldered. The workshop is lit by windows of this type.

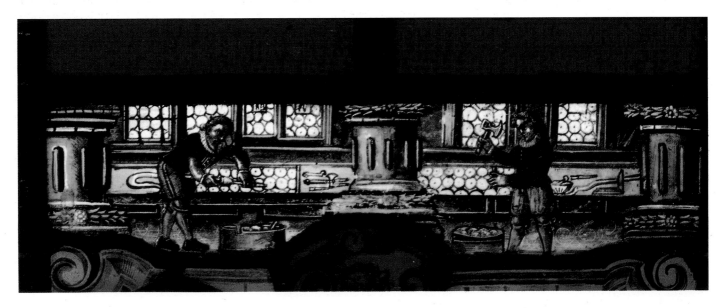

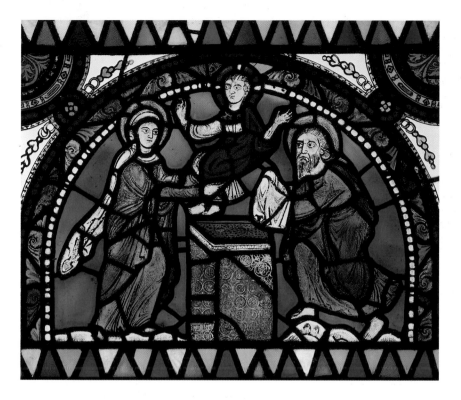

52 The Presentation of Christ in the Temple, originally in the Infancy Window of *c*.1144 at Saint-Denis near Paris but now in the parish church at Twycross, Leicestershire. The figures are placed against a brilliant blue background of sapphire blue soda glass. The glass outside the semi-circle is nineteenth-century.

century glazier is shown at work on a decorative panel of bull's eye glass; such use of crown glass was popular for both ecclesiastical and domestic windows in the fifteenth and sixteenth centuries, and is often depicted in Italian, German and Netherlandish paintings and prints of the period. Glazing of this kind, both under construction and installed in windows, can be seen in an exceptional panel of late sixteenth-century Swiss glass at Kreuzenstein Castle in Austria, a rare depiction of the interior of a glazier's workshop.

Many of the qualities of a medieval stained glass window depended on the qualities of the glass available to the glass-painter. Hand-blown window glass varies in thickness and texture; bubbles and impurities in the material give it a life and variety so obviously lacking in modern machine-made glass. Considering for how many centuries medieval glass has been keeping out wind and rain it is a remarkably resilient material, but because of the high alkali content from the beech-ash mixed with the sand, most medieval glass is prone to corrosion and pitting, as rain-water and condensation provide the conditions that will chemically attack it. There was little the glass-painter could have done about this problem, although glass excavated from buildings demolished in the Middle Ages proves that pitting was already damaging the exterior surface while it was still *in situ*.

Some medieval glass has remained remarkably stable. The most famous example is the twelfth-century blue – Suger's sapphire glass, the *bleu de ciel* of Chartres, also used at York – which is rich in soda and therefore much more stable than the more usual potash glass. The glass historian Eva Frodl-Kraft has drawn attention to a special green glass used east of the Rhine, whose high lead content has protected it from decay. Glass-making processes were certainly changing during the course of the Middle Ages and the availability of thinner, more transparent material in the late medieval period had a huge impact on what medieval glass-painters could do.

Colour was an important consideration in medieval notions of aesthetics; perhaps more than any other artist the glass-painter could exploit this love of colour to the full. It needs emphasising, however, that apart from small additions made by the glass-painter himself, the colours admired so much in medieval windows were already imparted at the glass-house when metallic oxides such as cobalt, copper and manganese were added to the molten glass. Theophilus makes it clear that the temperature of the kiln and the extent of the oxidisation would also affect the colour. Given impurities in the sand and problems of temperature control, the colours was likely to be a little unpredictable at times. Because the metallic oxides were added to the molten glass in clay pots, medieval coloured glasses are known as pot-metals, and the colour, with its characteristic depth and intensity, runs right through the thickness of the material. The thirteenth-century King Hezekiah panel from Canterbury is an excellent illustration of the medieval mosaic system with its combination of deeply coloured pot-metal glasses and lead, both carefully united so that

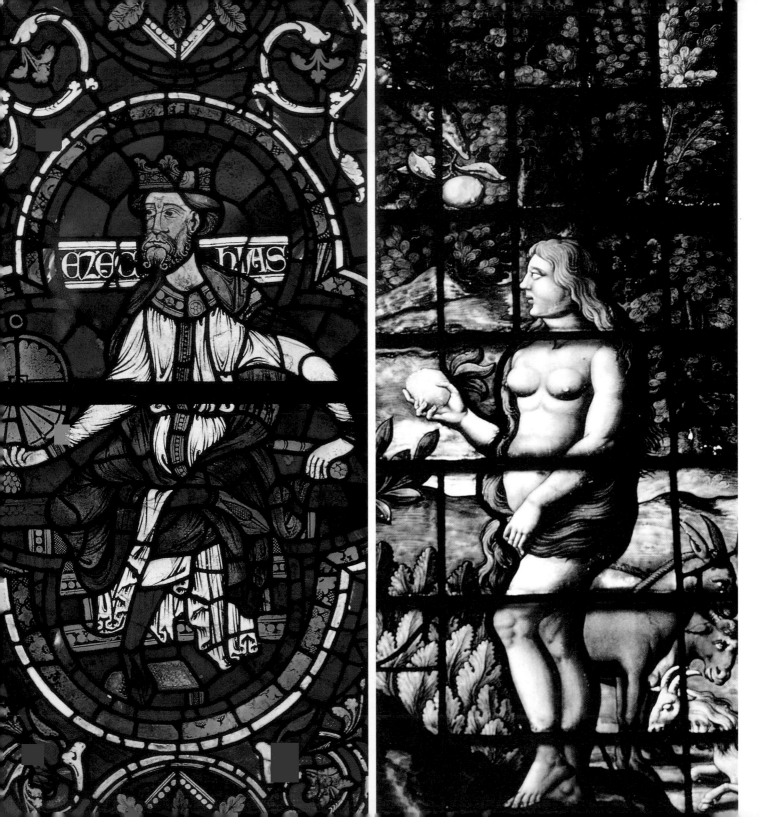

the image retains its clarity even when viewed from a distance. Comparison with a figure of Eve painted by Abraham van Linge in 1641 for University College, Oxford, should serve to underline the advantages of the medieval approach. The post-medieval window consists of a 'canvas' of white glass onto which the artist has painted vitreous enamel colours with a brush. Van Linge's colours are thin and opaque, and the painterly effects of light and shade contrast with the depth and transparency of colour used by the medieval artists. The lead plays a vital role in the Canterbury panel, enclosing the individual pieces of colour and reinforcing the design. In the seventeenth-century window the lead is virtually redundant from an artistic point of view; we are given the impression of looking down on Eden from a cell in the Bastille.

Most of the coloured glasses used by the medieval glass-painter were pot-metals, but an important exception was red, or ruby as it is commonly known. This colour is so intense at normal thickness that it would appear opaque or black. This problem was overcome by making a flashed-ruby, either by producing glass with a mixture of layers of white and red, or by blowing what is basically a white glass with a thin even coat of red on one surface. Some streaky rubies have such an interesting variety of colour that they can hold their own as a background without the addition of any painted ornament. Such ruby glass is used in the panel of Hezekiah from Canterbury and where the flashed glass is damaged, the base white glass can be seen. Red is the most common flashed glass to be used by the medieval glazier, but by the fifteenth century other colours such as flashed-green or blue can be found.

In histories of stained glass the medieval glass-maker tends to be a somewhat forgotten figure, but in the making of a stained glass window his role was crucial. Any artist has to work within the limitations of his materials and the move from the highly precocious jewel-like panels of the mid-twelfth century to the large transparent picture windows of the Renaissance to some extent depended on technical developments in the production of glass. Part of the glass-painter's art consisted of balancing and arranging colour; this might involve him in controlling the effects of light within a huge cathedral at one extreme, or choosing a single piece of coloured glass, perhaps a variegated blue, to suggest the shading in a drapery fold. In the Last Judgement window at Fairford in Gloucestershire, the work of Anglo-Netherland-ish artists of about 1500, Heaven is bathed in white and gold while the mouth of Hell is a brilliant exercise in different shades of flashed-ruby glass; not only do the glass-painters manage to suggest the flickering of flames, but by using thinly-flashed pieces they reproduce the white-hot intensity of the fire the damned must suffer.

By manually or mechanically grinding away the surface of the flashed glass the glazier could expose the white glass beneath to obtain two colours on one piece. An early, simple example of this technique, known as abrasion, was used to decorate a grisaille panel of c.1260 from the Cistercian monastery of Schulpforta in Germany. A fourteenth-century example from Lye on the Swedish island of Gotland shows abrasion used for Christ's cross-nimbus, the special halo that distinguishes him from the saints. At this small scale it would not have been feasible to lead in separate pieces of white glass without ruining the design. At Lye the abrasion was not totally successful but the artist thought it was worth taking a risk. Abrasion is most common on flashed-ruby glass, but towards the end of the Middle Ages as a greater range of flashed colours became available, its potential increased. The technique was particularly useful for complex heraldry, where too much lead would have obliterated the design. Some late medieval glass-painters became brilliant exponents of the technique, as a panel made in about 1480 for Kloster Nonnberg in Salzburg demonstrates. It was painted by the Peter Hemmel workshop and shows St Katherine in a richly brocaded robe, delicately abraded in flashed-ruby glass and reinforced with yellow stain. Abrasion is also used for the sleeves of the philosopher on the left of the canopy.

A good stock of coloured glass was obviously essential to the medieval glass-painter but one of the most crucial processes in making a

53 *Opposite, far left* King Hezekiah (Ezechias), one of a series of Christ's ancestors originally designed for the upper windows of the Trinity Chapel in Canterbury Cathedral in about 1220. This is a good example of the medieval pot-metal mosaic system with colour and lead combined to produce an image which could be read from a distance.

54 *Opposite* Eve in Paradise from a window depicting the Fall in the chapel of University College, Oxford. Painted by the Netherlandish glass-painter Abraham van Linge in 1641, the window was executed in coloured enamels and yellow stain on white glass. The painting techniques and grid-like leading contrast sharply with fig. 53.

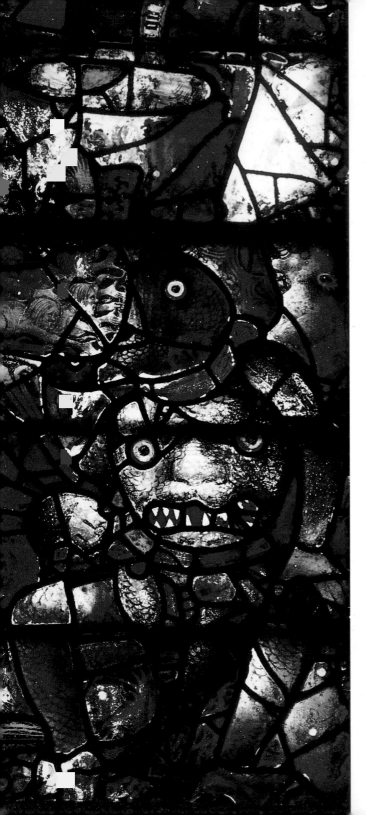

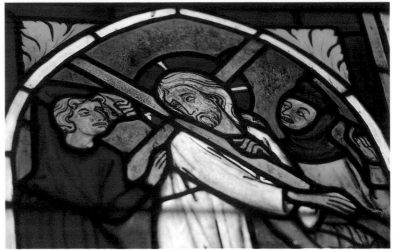

55 *Left* Hell Mouth, a detail of the Last Judgment in the west window of St Mary's Church, Fairford, Gloucestershire, painted by Anglo-Netherlandish artists around 1500. It is a technically brilliant exercise in flashed ruby glass and abrasion.

56 *Above* Christ carrying the Cross from Lye Church on the island of Gotland, Sweden. The panel, which dates from *c*.1325, shows abraded ruby glass being used for Christ's cross-nimbus.

stained glass window was the reinterpretation of the original sketch into a series of working drawings. A modern artist works from a paper cartoon, a highly finished drawing which usually shows the leadlines and the details to be painted on the glass. It can be hung up beside the glass-easel on which the stained glass artist paints his glass against the light. In a modern studio a separate cut-line drawing depicts the leadlines and indicates the colour to those who cut the glass. Laid out flat on the bench, the cut-line drawing represents the craft elements in the making of a window, as opposed to the more 'artistic' cartoon.

Working practices were very different for most of the medieval period when the full-scale working drawing was made directly onto a whitewashed table with the aid of a compass and ruler. Theophilus describes such a table in detail: the colours of the glass were indicated by letters so that cutting could take place on the table, and painted details, including highlights and shading were included, so that it was also used by those painting the glass and later on by those leading the panels. Documentary references to such tables can be found. At Windsor, for example, in 1351 Robert Russhmere was paid 9d. a day for 'drawing on the glazier's tables various designs' and contemporary accounts for St Stephen's Chapel, Westminster,

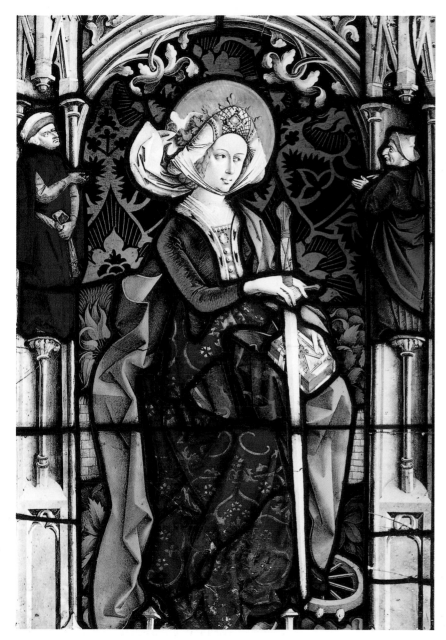

contain similar payments as well as a sum of 7d. 'For ale bought for washing the tables for designing glass'. An inventory of the contents of the glazing lodge at Westminster in 1443 mentions '2 portreying tables of waynescote'. Knowledge of such working methods was increased dramatically ten years ago with the discovery by the glass historian Joan Villa-Grau of two sections of a fourteenth-century table containing designs for windows in Girona Cathedral in Catalonia. These remarkable survivals assume extra importance because stained glass made from them is also extant, allowing comparisons of the two to be made. The Girona table, which shows evidence of reuse, contains designs for ornamental panels including an architectural canopy. It is a combination of cut- 58, 59 line and cartoon, and shows the marks of the nails which held the glass in place during leading. To save time, only essential painted detail is shown, leaving the rest to the common sense of the glass-painter who was thus allowed a certain amount of freedom. As Theophilus had advised, the designer used symbols to indicate colour to the glazier cutting the glass.

The use of tables explains much about the nature of glass-painting in the Middle Ages. The carrying out of the essential stages in the creation of a window on the one table imposed a certain discipline, and emphasises the craft element. But at the same time it underlines the unity of design and craft at this period, and suggests that the glass-painter enjoyed a certain amount of freedom and creativity when working on someone else's design. Medieval glass-painters have been criticised by some art historians for cutting corners and reusing designs, but drawing on the table was a highly skilled and complex process and it is not surprising that within one window or an extensive glazing scheme the designs on tables were reused or reversed. Occasionally there is evidence to suggest that the same table was used for windows in separate buildings. This was probably the case with two fourteenth-century Virgin and Child panels from Fladbury and Warndon some ten miles apart in Worcester- 61, 62 shire; basic measurements and cut-lines are the same although there are variations in colour and

57 St Katherine, made in about 1480 by the Strasbourg workshop of Peter Hemmel, was probably originally in Kloster Nonnberg in Salzburg, Austria. Abraded ruby glass is used with yellow stain for the saint's robe and the gown worn by the pagan philosopher on the left. The panel bears witness to the high artistic quality and technical brilliance of the Hemmel workshop.

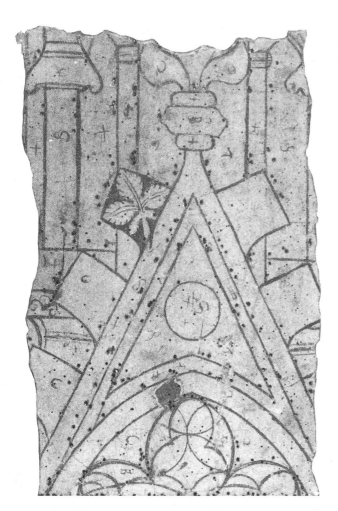

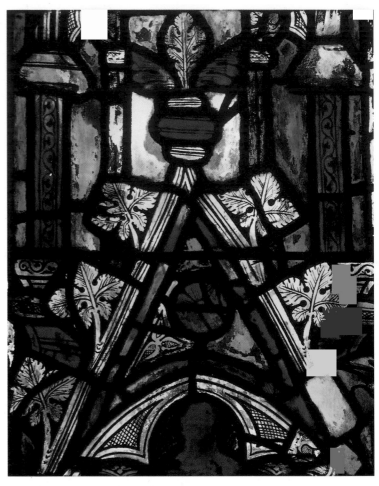

58 A detail of a canopy design (left) from a mid-fourteenth-century glazing table, used in the making of the windows of Girona Cathedral, Spain. The detail shows the marks of glazing nails and the colours indicated by letters and symbols, and it shows evidence of reuse.

59 The panel (right) is the original fourteenth-century canopy made on the glazing table.

ornament (see p.44). As measurements were likely to vary from window to window tables were not conserved but cleaned for reuse once the commission had been completed. At a time when paper was extremely expensive and parchment was the preferred medium for codices and records, the working table was a cheap and practical solution, but it was difficult to transport and it could not be stored very easily. The change towards cartoons as we know them today was probably a gradual one and a response to the greater availability of paper in Northern Europe during the fifteenth century. Life-size designs for glass on parchment from an

earlier period are extremely rare survivals. One such example, dating from the middle of the fourteenth century, is a drawing of St Katherine from Seitenstetten in Lower Austria, still bearing evidence of its use as a cartoon. In Italy paper was more widely used at an earlier date than in the north and in his *Libro dell' Arte*, Cennino Cennini says that stained glass cartoons should be made from sheets of paper glued together, with the figures drawn in charcoal and fixed in ink; they were to be spread out on the bench and used by the glazier cutting the glass. Cartoons dating from 1567 for the architect Pellegrino Tibaldi's masons window of

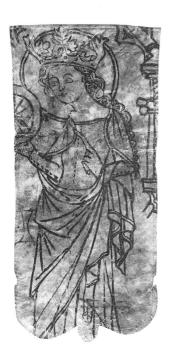

the Four Crowned Martyrs made by Corrado da Colonia (Konrad Much of Cologne) for the nave of Milan Cathedral are preserved in the Pinacoteca Ambrosiana and are the earliest surviving cartoons of their kind in Italy.

In England the Westminster inventory of 1443 lists '25 shields painted on paper with various arms of the King for patterns for the use of glaziers working there' and '6 crestis with various arms for the same works', which sound more like large-scale working drawings than the illuminated armorials on the roll provided to guide the glaziers working at Greenwich later in

the century. The wills of York glass-painters confirm that drawings of some sort were handed on to their successors. The drawings (*protractoria*) bequeathed by Thomas Shirley in 1456 and William English's workshop drawings (*picturis opelle*) of 1480 may have been small in scale, but when Robert Preston bequeathed 'all my scrowles' to Thomas English in 1503 and John Petty his *'scroes'* to his brother Robert in 1508, they seem to have been referring to rolled-up cartoons. Certainly cartoons became the standard form of window design in the sixteenth century. An inventory of the workshop of the

60 *Above* Parchment cartoon from the middle of the fourteenth century from Seitenstetten, Austria. The design is for a small-scale figure of St Katherine standing under a canopy.

61, 62 *Right* Two panels dating from *c*.1330–40 from the parish churches of Fladbury (left) and Warndon (right), both in Worcestershire. They were made by the same local atelier, reusing a design on a table like that preserved in Girona (figs.58, 59).

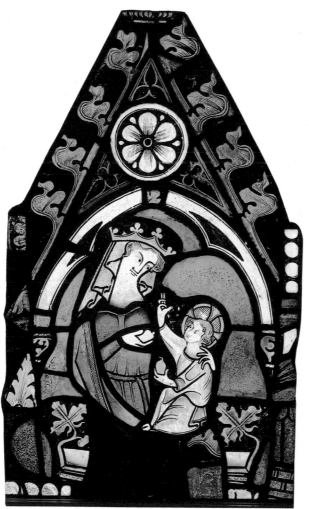

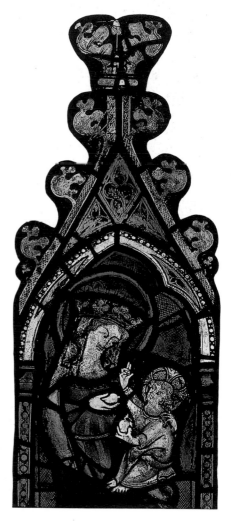

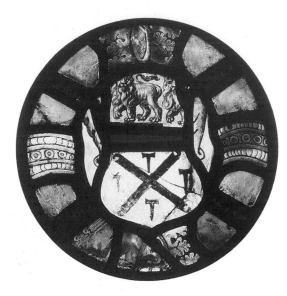

63 Arms of the York Glaziers Guild in a panel of *c.*1530 in the Guild Church of St Helen, York. The shield consists of two grozing irons, used for cutting glass, and four glazing nails, used to fix the glass to the bench. The lions above are a later intrusion.

Parisian glass-painter Laurent Marchant, made after his death in 1579, mentions 'several large cartoons on paper which were used to make church windows', and there is a similar entry in the inventory made after Nicholas Pinaigrier's death in 1606. The scarcity of such references in Parisian inventories is not particularly surprising; presumably glass-painters were not interested in preserving cartoons once they had been used. What is exceptional is the survival of the sixteenth-century cartoons used to make the famous windows in St Jan's Church, Gouda, in the years following 1555. These were deliberately and carefully preserved in the church archives with an eye to future conservation and repairs to the windows.

Once the design had been laid out on the table or cartoon the glass had to be cut to the appropriate shapes. Medieval glaziers used a method described by Theophilus in which the glass was cracked with a hot iron and its edges trimmed into shape with a grozing iron. This had a hook at each end and left a characteristic 'nibbled' edge which can be seen when the glass is removed from the lead. Such tools are mentioned frequently in documents. At Windsor in 1351 Simon le Smyth was paid 1d. each for twelve grozing irons *(croisures)*, and the York glass-painter Robert Preston left 'iij grosyng

yrnes' to Thomas English in 1503. A patched shield of about 1530 in St Helen's Church, York, depicts the arms of the local Guild of Glaziers which consists of glazing nails between two grozing irons crossed in saltire. Cutting glass in this way must have been a long and delicate process, but medieval glaziers were capable of extremely skilful cutting, even removing circles or lozenges from larger pieces of glass.

Exactly when the diamond was first used for cutting glass is not known, but it was used by the fourteenth century in Italy and is mentioned with other hard stones in Antonio da Pisa's treatise. Diamond-cutting is a more convenient method, which leaves a straighter edge, and seems to have spread gradually during the course of the sixteenth century, and must have been especially useful for cutting plain quarry glazing.

Once the glass was cut there followed perhaps the most skilful operation of all, the actual painting of the glass itself. This process is illustrated in the Gerlachus panel from Munster. The pigment used can vary in colour from grey to reddish brown or dark black and consisted of a mixture of iron oxide (Theophilus recommends copper), glass as a flux, and gum arabic, urine or wine as a binder. It was the only colour (with the exception of yellow stain from the fourteenth century onwards), which the glass-painter applied to the glass, until the addition of certain carnation and sanguine colours in the late fifteenth century, and the introduction of coloured enamels in the sixteenth century.

The paint, which in English documents is often referred to as *geet* or *arnement* because of its blackness, was applied to the glass with a variety of brushes made from badger, squirrel and other animal furs. No doubt medieval glass-painters, like their modern counterparts, used other methods of spreading paint; indeed, it is clear that some of the painters who worked with Master Robert on the west window of York Minster in 1339 used their fingers in places. Sticks, needles or even the end of a brush could be used to scratch away painted areas to produce ornament in reserve or highlights. Although most of the paint was applied to the inner surface of the glass, back-painting on the

64 Cartoons on paper with designs of the Baptism of Christ for a section of the east window of St Jan's Church, Gouda. The glass was given by George van Egmond, Bishop of Utrecht, and was made by the workshop of Dirck Crabeth in 1555. These full-scale working drawings, which follow the individual lights, indicate the designs to be followed by the glass-painters, as well as the main horizontal divisions of the leadlines and saddlebars. The survival of so many of the cartoons for the Gouda windows gives the church a very special place in the history of glass-painting.

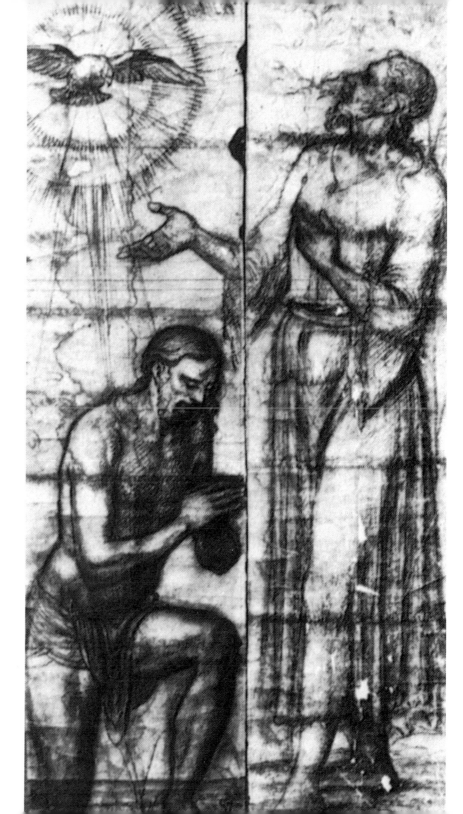

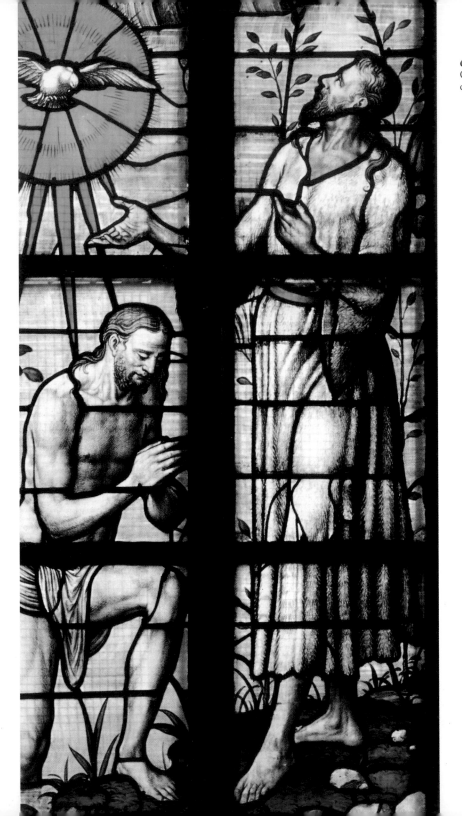

65 Detail of the east window of St Jan's Church, Gouda, showing the stained glass made from the cartoon illustrated in fig.64.

exterior was commonly used in the Middle Ages, either to reinforce shading on the inner surface, or for special effects. In a fifteenth-century donor panel from Waterperry, Oxfordshire, for example, hair has been painted on the outside of the glass to give the viewer the illusion of looking through a transparent veil.

The painting would have been done with the glass flat on the bench and without the aid of the glass-easels used today. Main painted outlines were applied in thick *trace-lines*, with a thick, even black *matting* for reserve work, and different types of modelling for flesh or drapery; *smear-shading* which consisted of even washes of thin solutions of paint, or, from the mid-fourteenth century, *stipple-shading* in which the paint was dabbed with the end of a hard brush allowing greater translucency. The painting carries all the details of the design, ornament and shading, but it has a practical function too in carefully modulating the light. Theophilus gives a clear account of twelfth-century painting techniques:

When you have made your strokes of the aforesaid colour on the draperies, spread the colour with the paintbrush so that the glass is clear in that part where you normally make highlights in a painting. And let the brush strokes be thick in one place, light in another and then lighter, and distinguished with such care that they give the appearance of three shades of colour being applied. You ought also to follow this procedure below the eyebrows and around the eyes, nostrils and chin, about the faces of young men, and around bare feet and hands and other parts of the nude body. It should have the appearance of a painting composed of a variety of colours.

Twelfth-century windows like those at Saint-Denis or Chartres show exactly this approach, indeed the famous head from Wissembourg of the previous century has the same tonal qualities. Gothic glass-painters were less hieratic in approach, indeed glass-painting techniques responded to a desire for more naturalism as time went on. The head of Edward the Confessor from York Minster, possibly the work of John Thornton, is an excellent example of early fifteenth-century glass-painting techniques. The artist has used very fine brushes, cross-hatching, stippling and stickwork to create a sophisticated image in the soft style so fashionable at this

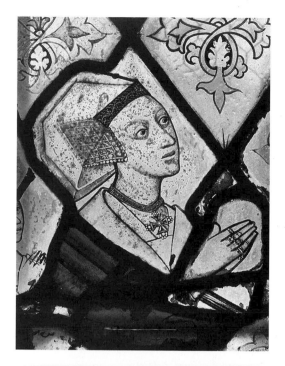

66 Detail of Margaret Fitz Ellis, donor of a window dated 1461–9 in Waterperry Church, Oxfordshire. It shows a variety of painting techniques including stipple shading and scratching out. The upper part of the lozenge on the headdress has been painted on the back of the glass to create the illusion of a transparent veil.

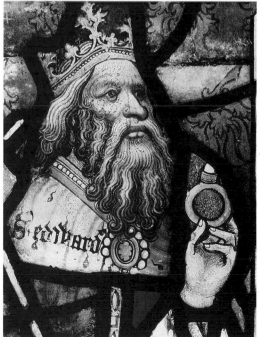

67 Head of St Edward the Confessor, one of the twenty-four legendary and historic figures from the bottom row of the east window of York Minster made by John Thornton and his workshop between 1405 and 1408. A variety of painting techniques including fine-line drawing, smear shading, stipple shading, cross-hatching and scratching out, has been used to create this expressive head which may be the work of Thornton himself.

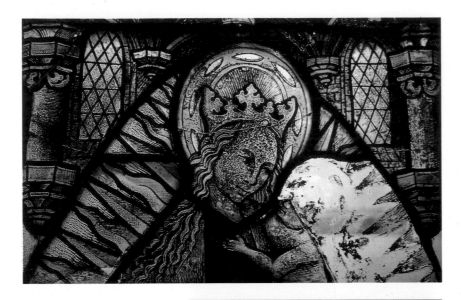

date. The painting techniques of Theophilus and Thornton were in their different ways very demanding and time consuming. It may have been partially to speed the process up, and partially to achieve greater naturalism that later medieval glass-painters laid more emphasis on stipple-shading. The Virgin and Child panel, 68 painted around 1500 and originally in Holmstrup church in Denmark, is typical of work all over Europe at this time. Northern glass-painters, possibly emulating Netherlandish panel-painting, began to experiment, not always successfully, with their paint. Such experimentation led to the introduction in the 1530s of the radically different vitreous enamel colours which were ultimately to threaten the technical tradition within which the medieval glass-painter worked.

In order to fix the painted detail to the surface of the glass permanently it had to be fired in a kiln at a temperature of about 600 to 620° Centigrade. Theophilus describes a small kiln made out of arched rods covered with clay and horse dung into which the glass was placed on beds of dry quick-lime or ashes in iron trays. At Guildford Castle in 1292 8d. was paid for a

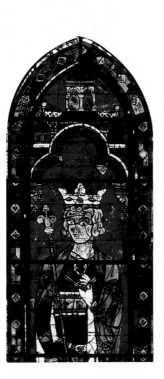

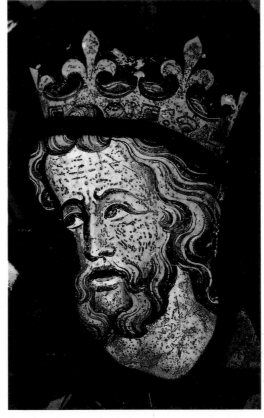

68 *Top* The Virgin and Child, now in the National Museum, Copenhagen, is executed almost entirely in white glass and yellow stain and with a predominately stipple-shaded painting technique typical of much stained glass made around 1500. The detailed architectural setting includes representations of little windows glazed with quarries.

69 *Far left* King Solomon from the south transept of Chartres Cathedral. This window was made between 1221 and 1230, long before the invention of yellow stain. All the yellow pieces are pot-metal colours and have had to be individually leaded in.

70 *Left* Head of Christ, detail of a window of *c.*1340 in St Mary Castlegate, York. Using the technique of yellow stain the glass-painter has been able to produce a gold beard, hair and crown on what was originally a single piece of glass.

71 *Opposite* A clerical donor before St Peter, dating from 1313, from the parish church of Le Mesnil-Villeman (Manche) in France. This is the earliest firmly-dated example of the yellow stain technique used extensively here to colour white glass yellow and blue glass green.

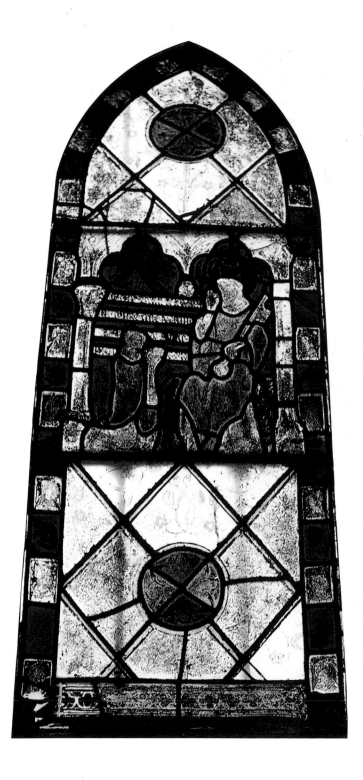

furnace made for burning glass' which was fuelled by brushwood from the surrounding park. Heinrich Oidtmann calculated that it would take about six hours for a wood fire to reach the required temperature, and some twelve hours for the gradual cooling of the clay walls. Proper firing was essential if the paint was to last and, not surprisingly, it is often mentioned in contracts. In 1547 when the glass-painter Jacques Aubry was working for the church of St-Nicholas-des-Champs in Paris, the contract insisted that the paint should be 'bonne et bien recuite'. Some medieval glass-painters were apparently prepared to add some cold pigment to the glass after firing. Cennino Cennini recommends oil paint dried in the sun for very small-scale work and there is a recipe in an English fifteenth-century manuscript in the Huntingdon Library, San Marino, (formerly in the collection of Reginald Rawden Hastings) 'To make curyus worke on glasse wyndowes after the be aneled' which also uses an oil medium.

Yellow stain was another technique which involved painting and firing. By applying a liquid solution of silver nitrate or sulphide to the exterior surface (there are several references to the purchase of silver filings for the windows of St Stephen's Chapel, Westminster, in 1351–2) the glass-painter could turn white glass yellow and, more rarely, blue glass green, by firing it in the kiln. In the Middle Ages one firing may have been used for both paint and stain and the tone could vary from pale yellow to deep orange depending on the amount of stain, the quality of the glass and the temperature of the firing. Yellow stain was discovered early in the fourteenth century, allowing, for example, a head of 70 Christ of about 1340 from York to have a gold crown, halo, hair and beard on what was originally a single piece of white glass, when previously, as in the thirteenth-century figure of Solomon at Chartres the hair, brooch, part of the 69 sceptre and border pieces, had to be cut from sheets of pot-metal yellow glass. According to Jean Lafond, the earliest dated example of the yellow stain technique is a panel in the tiny 71 church of Le Mesnil-Villeman in Normandy, where a rather faded inscription contains the

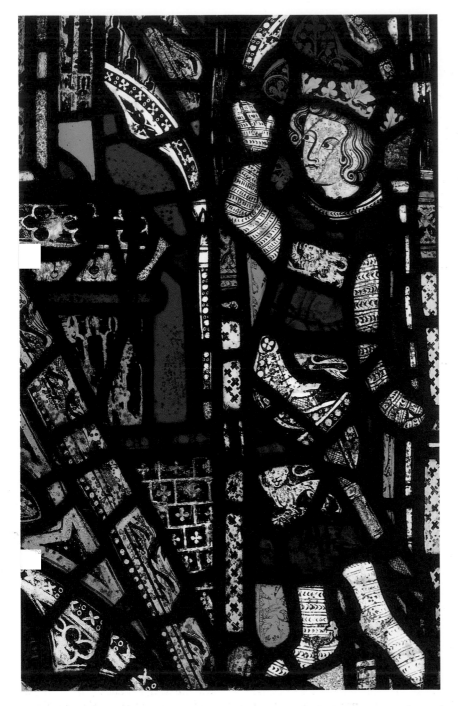

date 1313. Doubtless, stain had previously been used in such major glass-painting centres as Paris and Rouen, and it was used by English glaziers at about the same time – for example in the borders of the Heraldic Window at York Minster, given by Canon Peter de Dene, probably between 1307 and 1310. Here, stain is used with great skill to enhance the armour and fittings of the King of England, one of the [72] heraldic figures in the borders of the window, although some of the original colour has been removed by corrosion. The technique allowed glass-painters to explore new aesthetic approaches with increasing use of white glass producing much lighter and brighter buildings. By the second quarter of the fourteenth century whole panels, even whole windows could be executed virtually entirely in white glass and stain. This not only had its effect on church interiors at places like Cologne, Rouen, Ely or York, but it was particularly important in domestic settings where roundels and squares using yellow stain would allow imagery without in any way diminishing the light.

Much of the medieval glass-painter's skill went into elaborate ornamentation of windows; besides techniques described above, such as use of yellow stain or elaborate cutting and leading, there were other methods of adding jewel-like colour. Theophilus wrote a whole section on 'Setting Gems in Painted Glass' in which he describes a rare technique, called annealing by glass historians, by which small jewels of coloured glass could be fixed on drapery, haloes and other parts of a window without the use of leads. These were placed on the glass to be decorated and held in place by painting a thick [75] layer of paint around them and firing them in the kiln. According to Theophilus 'they will stick so firm that they will never fall out', but surviving examples show that he was an optimist. An

72 The King of England from a canopy in the Heraldic Window of *c.*1307–10 in the nave of York Minster. Pot-metal yellow is used for the lions, crown and architecture but yellow stain is used for the spurs, armour and sword fittings, in what is one of the earliest surviving examples of the technique in England.

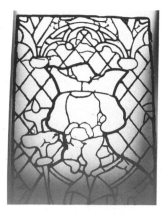

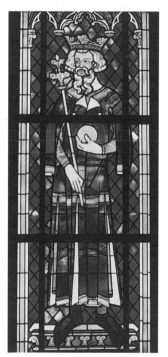

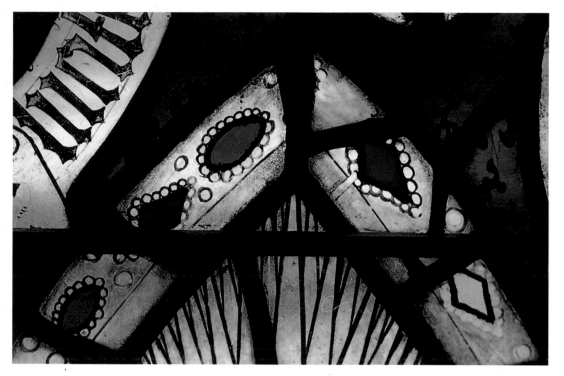

73, 74 The original lead (above left) of the upper part of the figure (left) for an Old Testament King dating from *c.*1315 in the choir clerestory of Cologne Cathedral in Germany. In a medieval window the lead not only kept the glass in place but helped to carry the overall design. It was cast and produced in different thicknesses in order to give emphasis to particularly important features. The original lead was replaced in 1972.

75 *Above* Detail of a jewelled mandorla (oval halo) from an early fifteenth-century window in St Michael Spurriergate, York. The annealing technique used here is mentioned by Theophilus. Most of the jewels have remained in place but the one at the bottom right has fallen out.

early example of the technique, though a century after Theophilus, can be seen in the Jesse window of about 1230 in Regensburg Cathedral, where the border to the left of the Kings of Judah has blue glass for amethysts with tiny abraded pieces of ruby, only some of which survive. The technique was used at Klosterneuburg near Vienna in the fourteenth century and there are three examples dating between about 1375 and 1430 in York.

A more secure and hence more common method of embellishing glass was simply to integrate the jewel into the leading as, for example, at Augsburg. The very precocious effects created by John Prudde's workshop at the Beauchamp Chapel in Warwick depend in part on this simple solution, but some jewels have been leaded into small holes carefully drilled through the glass.

Once the painted glass had been fired it was returned to the table to be leaded together. Occasionally, for large glazing schemes, sorting marks painted or scratched out of pigment had previously been applied to the glass so that the craftsmen leading the panels could easily distinguish pieces belonging together. Lead plays a vital role in a medieval window, not merely holding the individual pieces of glass in place,

73, 74

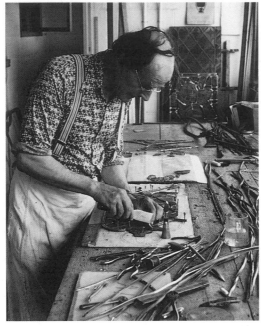

76 *Right* Alec King of G. King and Sons, Norwich, releading a panel of medieval glass. The glass is being assembled over a cutline drawing. On the bench are long strips of milled leads which replaced the cast leads used in the Middle Ages.

77 *Below* An exterior view of the ambulatory of Canterbury Cathedral, taken in 1942 when the windows were removed for safety, showing the thirteenth-century iron armatures (ferramenta) which help to support the glass and structure the composition.

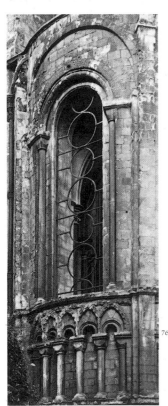

but helping to emphasise the basic design. Because of breakages and crude releading over the centuries it is often difficult to appreciate the artistic skill which went into the positioning of the original leading which could vary in thickness within one panel. Medieval lead cames were cast in moulds by the glaziers themselves, a process described by Theophilus, and were H-shaped in section with straight or rounded profiles. The introduction of lead mills in the sixteenth century allowed for longer, thinner and more supple leads and would have saved the glaziers a lot of time. However, the old cast leads were stronger and more serviceable and although most medieval windows have been re-leaded several times, there is still a surprising number of panels, mostly on the Continent, which are either still in the original leading, or where the original leading has only been replaced in recent times.

76   The leads are bent to the shape of the glass, cut and soldered up into individual panels. Tin and mutton fat for soldering are commonly mentioned in glazing accounts, along with 'soudyngirens' themselves. Such tools can be

seen in Jost Amman's woodcut of a glazing workshop, one of them being heated in a brazier. Made watertight, the finished panels were ready to be transported to the site and fixed into the stonework.

Although the manufacture of the ferramenta, the ironwork used to support the weight of the glass and lead in its architectural framework, was the responsibility of a smith, it was the glazier's job to see that the panels were properly fixed, a responsibility underlined in several medieval glazing contracts.

In the large single openings of early windows from the twelfth and the first half of the thirteenth century, quite complex iron armatures were used. Their function was load bearing, but they also gave overall design, order and 77 pattern to a window as any visitor to Canterbury, Chartres or the Sainte-Chapelle in Paris can see. With the development of multi-light traceried windows during the course of the thirteenth century the main light glazing tended to be simplified into rectangular panels supported by T-bars and crossed at regular intervals by smaller saddlebars (*soudelett* in English accounts) attached to the panels by little lead strips.

The making of a stained glass window consisted of a series of stages – choice of glass, cutting, painting, firing, leading, fixing – any of which could go wrong. Many of the surviving medieval panels are still in high positions, keeping out the wind and the rain after centuries, despite the neglect or even ill-treatment they have experienced even in recent times. They bear eloquent testimony to the craftsmen who produced them, and to the traditional methods they employed. Given the multiplicity of tasks to be done and the often collaborative nature of medieval window production, planning and precision were of the essence. The success of a medieval workshop depended on a high level of organisation by the master in charge. To judge by the results, simple tools and basic technology were no inhibition to artistic ability, yet painting a window in the Middle Ages must have involved an act of faith for the glass-painters then could hardly have been able to judge the outcome of much of their work until the scaffolding finally came down.

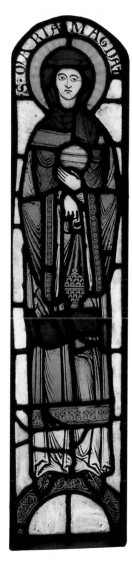

78 A small-scale but imposing figure of St Mary Magdalen dating from *c.*1160–70. It was probably originally located in the Baptismal Chapel of St John and St Mary Magdalen at Weitensfeld in Austria.

In order to provide a context for the medieval glass-painter this book began with a chapter giving the background to the rise of stained glass as an artistic medium. This concluding chapter attempts to account for the radical changes which affected glass-painters during the course of the sixteenth century, as the traditions which had sustained them over the centuries collapsed. To avoid simple and convenient but also misleading ideas of period, this book takes its account of the medieval glass-painter down to the middle of the sixteenth century, a period of actual significance in the history of the art, for it acknowledges the technical innovations taking place in stained glass and the historical development of the medium, especially as it was affected by the religious upheavals of the time. For the glass-painter the years around 1550 were much more crucial than the years around 1500.

When it was fashionable for historians to look upon the late Middle Ages as an era which showed civilisation in decline, art historians regarded glass as an art that mirrored that decay. Nineteenth-century artists and critics, anxious to restore the craft to its former glory, went through the complete range of medieval styles in rapid succession. Although there was a reaction against medievalism in certain circles in the 1860s, the best models that were held up to contemporary artists dated from the early Middle Ages. Twelfth-century glass-painters tended to be a little primitive for nineteenth-century taste, while sixteenth-century artists were held to be over refined, even decadent, their windows being too pictorial for what was essentially an architectural art, and their classical ornament having dangerous associations with paganism. The Victorians settled for a middle course based on the style which had flourished in the years around 1300. The glass historian Jean Lafond spent a lifetime rehabilitating French glass-painters of the first half of the sixteenth century from the ideological and aesthetic prejudices of previous generations. A dispassionate assessment of windows produced during this period makes it difficult to accept the nineteenth-century prejudices against the work of late medieval glass-painters.

It is true that many craftsmen at the time retained a traditional approach to the medium; basic techniques were not radically different from those described by Theophilus, and the guilds which were structured to protect glaziers from outside competition, no doubt helped to maintain the artistic as well as the economic *status quo*. However, patrons and institutions found ways of circumventing obstacles to change and leading designers and glass-painters were remarkably mobile in the sixteenth century, more so than many of their modern counterparts despite the Common Market. Artists like Guillaume de Marcillat and Konrad Much could move from France and Germany to Italy, or from the Netherlands to France, like Arnold of Nijmegen, from Germany and the Netherlands to England like Galyon Hone and Barnard Flower or even from England to the Netherlands like the glazier Albert Stope who left Colchester for 's Hertogensbosch in Brabant in 1558. There was clearly no shortage of patronage all over Europe in the early sixteenth century and stained glass, far from undergoing recession, seems to have been open to technical experimentation, stylistic change and business enterprise.

It is easy to see why the directness, technical brilliance and intense jewel-like qualities of the works of twelfth-century glass-painters were admired so much in the nineteenth century. Just such qualities can be seen in a small St Mary Magdalen window of *c.*1160–70 from Weitensfeld in Austria. This is executed in rather simple colours, with elegant drapery and delicate ornament; considering the size of the panel (0.38 m by 0.13 m) it is a remarkably imposing and monumental work of art. However, equally, glass-painters working nearly 500 years later

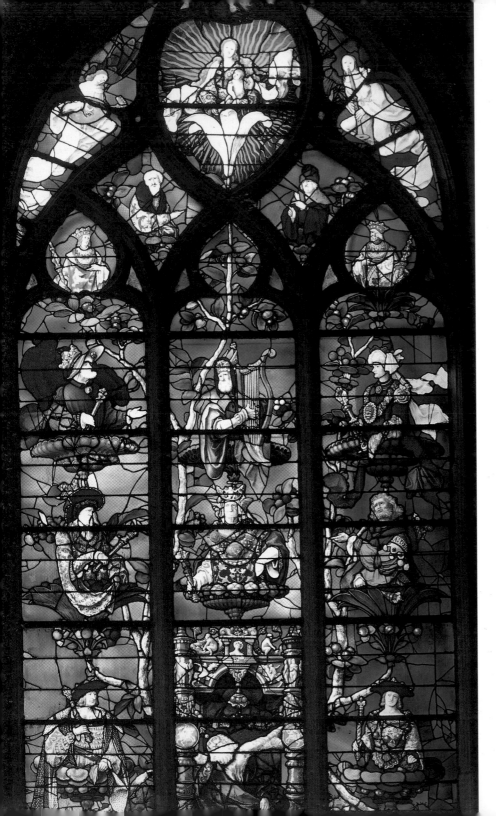

showed great technical ability and mastery in exploiting the medium to the full. The figure of Solomon from the Jesse window painted in 79 about 1525 by the Le Prince family for the church of Saint-Etienne in Beauvais helps to reinforce this point. Despite a little damage, the king, who emerges from a flower set against a brilliant blue background, is a technical *tour de force* in the use of abraded ruby glass and yellow stain. The panel illustrates the stylistic changes that were current across Europe at this date, as northern glass-painters responded in different ways to the art and architecture of the Italian Renaissance. This influence can be seen in the exotic form of the winged crown with putto worn by Solomon, in the heavy metallic floral swag that hangs around his neck, and in the classical design of the sceptre which he holds in his right hand. The Beauvais window exudes confidence and shows little sign of an art form in crisis, let alone in terminal decline.

Although, as discussed above, the general methods used by medieval glass-painters remained fairly stable, the sixteenth century saw experimentation in painting itself which, it has been argued, led to the total collapse of traditional techniques. By the 1530s glass-painters had begun experimenting with vitreous enamel pigments with metallic oxide colouring agents which had long been in use as a means of decorating vessel glass. Artists could now paint colour directly onto white glass instead of leading in translucent pot-metal colours. Both the manufacture of the enamels and their successful firing were fraught with difficulties; their origins remain obscure. Like many artistic experiments in other media, it is possible that they were first used in the Netherlands. Blue seems to have been the first colour employed; there are examples from Antwerp which can be dated to around 1538. An early English example is a small Tudor crown with jewels in blue enamel to be seen in St Michael-le-Belfrey,

79 The spectacular Jesse Window, a genealogical tree showing Christ's earthly and spiritual ancestors, in the church of Saint-Etienne in Beauvais. It was made in about 1525 by the workshop of Engrand Le Prince, who appears in the guise of a prophet on the right of the second row. Alongside him in the centre light is the exotic figure of Solomon, illustrating the influence of the Italian Renaissance on French stained glass design.

York, and which probably belongs to the glazing scheme of *c*.1540. Early examples in France are probably the work of Parisian glass-painters; blue enamel is used in an Infancy of Christ window of 1543 at Monfort l'Amaury (Yvelines) and violet is also introduced in the *Ecce Homo* window painted for the same church in the following year. Yellow stain could be combined with blue enamel to create green (a green enamel was in use in Switzerland in the 1590s) and it was not long before a whole range of different colours was in use.

For monumental windows in ecclesiastical settings the effects of the new pigments were hardly revolutionary; not really appropriate for large-scale works, they were used discreetly at first in subsidiary areas of the design. It was not until the 1560s that they began to appear regularly in large windows; the first such dated example in a Parisian church is in a window of 1568 in Saint-Etienne-du-Mont. Although supplies of pot-metal glass became scarcer works as late as the seventeenth century by the Van Linge family from Emden or by Henry Gyles of York were often executed in a mixture of pot-metal and enamel painted techniques.

Where enamels were really influential was in small-scale domestic stained glass where the use of white glass and less lead was appropriate and where the opacity of the pigments, used in miniature, was less of a disadvantage. Used on roundels, ovals and small rectangles, enamels came into their own and Netherlandish and Swiss glass-painters developed them into a fine art, as a landscape panel of the Temptation of Christ by the Zurich artist Hans Nüscheler in Darmstadt shows. Religious subjects remained extremely popular with enamel glass-painters, but so too were heraldic, mythological and domestic scenes; many of the designs were copied from prints and engravings.

It is possible that the glass-painters developed the enamels in response to the ever increasing demand for domestic glazing. While

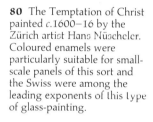

80 The Temptation of Christ painted *c*.1600–16 by the Zürich artist Hans Nüscheler. Coloured enamels were particularly suitable for small-scale panels of this sort and the Swiss were among the leading exponents of this type of glass-painting.

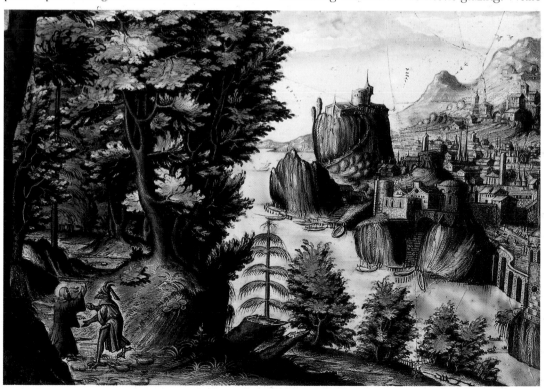

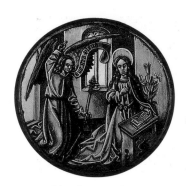

81 The Annunciation, a Netherlandish roundel of *c*.1500 in Longleat House, Wiltshire.

this demand was led from the top, with heraldic displays in Tudor palaces in England, or the glazing for Francois I's palace of Fontainbleau (1527 and following), or the Story of Psyche windows formerly in the Château at Ecouen (1542–4), it filtered downwards and, in the Netherlands and Switzerland, became almost a popular art.

It is not easy to document the increased output in domestic glazing during the sixteenth century but recent research in France has shown that clients of Parisian glass-painters included not only the king and the nobles, but merchants and artisans who commissioned glass both for their homes and their shops. The increase in domestic consumption, both of stained glass and especially of plain glazing, may well have contributed to the lessening of interest in monumental church windows. It was clearly a major factor in the process, already described, leading to the break up of an integrated glazing craft into specialised components – the increased demand for plain glazing being satisfied by glaziers and domestic stained glass commissions being carried out by a small number of glass-painters who had learned the secrets of enamels.

Change in fashion was one of the most important factors which determined the market for monumental stained glass. As a creation of the Middle Ages it was closely allied to Gothic architecture and as classical forms came to the fore, demand for stained glass inevitably waned. Some monumental glass was produced in England, France and the Netherlands during the seventeenth century, but not a lot. Even in Catholic countries which avoided the Reformation, the great days of the glass-painters were over. The architecture of the Counter Reformation was baroque in style and the statuary and painted vaults of its church interiors demanded plain glazing.

Another decisive blow to glass-painters in the sixteenth century was the devastating effect of the Reformation leading to the break up of the medieval Catholic Church. Long before this there had been opponents to stained glass on religious grounds. In the twelfth century St Bernard of Clairvaux and the reformed order of Cistercian monks had prohibited coloured and figurative glazing in their churches. This austere and seemingly negative response had nevertheless produced some of the most simple and beautiful ornamented grisaille panels by medieval glaziers. Heretical groups such as the Cathars or the followers of John Wyclif in England, known as Lollards, attacked the institutional church and its fabric and regarded costly and beautiful works of art such as stained glass windows as snares of the devil. When later Protestant reformers attacked Rome, the cult of saints, relics, pilgrimage and the monasteries, an art form which was bound up with religious orthodoxy inevitably came under attack.

Although attacks on images varied in intensity – Luther himself was rather tolerant, while Karlstadt, Calvin and Zwingli took a much harder line – iconoclasm became an important element in Protestant ideology, at times able to force the speed of theological change. In the period between 1521, the date of iconoclastic attacks in Wittenberg, and the middle of the century, destruction took place not only in countries like Germany, Switzerland, the Netherlands, the British Isles and, to a lesser extent, Scandinavia, where Protestants held power, but also in Catholic countries like France, which suffered severely during the religious wars.

In England iconoclasm was to a large extent directed by government control and under a royal proclamation of 1538 it was left to individual bishops to interpret the law on images. However, once Henry VIII had moved against the greater monasteries in 1539, shrines were demolished, churches pulled down and vast quantities of glass destroyed. A painting in the National Portrait Gallery in London shows the King on his deathbed handing over the Protestant succession to his son Edward VI supported by his counsellors Archbishop Cranmer and Lord Protector Somerset. It is a crude but effective piece of anti-Papal propaganda, echoing Cranmer's words at the coronation of the boy king, enjoining him to be 'Christ's vicar within your dominions, and to see, with your predecessor Josias, God truly worshipped and idolatory destroyed – the tyranny of the Bishops of Rome banished from your subjects

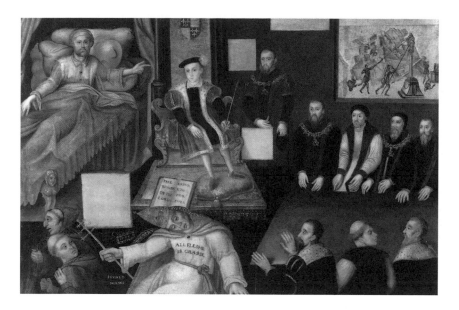

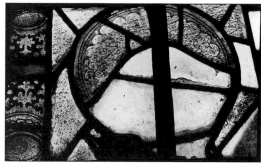

82 *Left* Edward VI and the Pope, an oil painting of c.1548 by an unknown artist. It is blatant anti-Catholic propaganda. As Henry VIII hands the Protestant succession to his son, soldiers pull down the monasteries and break images. The biblical word is shown triumphing over 'Feigned Holiness' and 'Idolatry'.

83 *Above* Damaged head of a saint from a fifteenth-century window in Slimbridge Church, Gloucestershire. At the Reformation such iconoclasm was widespread.

and images removed'. Indeed in the picture the Pope is vanquished and in the background monasteries and statues are razed to the ground.

At such a time of destruction stained glass was something of a privileged medium when compared with other works of art; wall-paintings could be scraped or whitewashed, sculpture could be smashed or removed, but stained glass had an extra function since it kept the elements out of the building. As one contemporary Englishman put it:

whiche ben the most profytable sayntes in the chyrche? – They that stonde in the glasse windows, for they keep out the wynd for wastynge of the lyghte.

William Harrison in his famous *Description of England* published in 1577, makes much the same point:

Monuments of idolatrie are removed, taken downe and defaced; onlie the stories in glasse windowes excepted, which for want of sufficient store of newe stuffe, and by reason of extreame charge that should grow by the alteration of the same into white panes throughout the realme, are not altogither abolished in most places at once, but by little and little suffered to decaie, that white glasse may be provided and set up in their roomes.

Particularly offensive imagery in windows was no doubt removed – in 1525 in Stralsund on the Baltic coast of Germany, for example, all the figural glazing in the town is said to have been buried in the cemetery of St Catherine's Convent – but usually more economical methods sufficed. In Slimbridge in Gloucestershire a fifteenth-century saint underwent a second martyrdom when an iconoclast 'neutralised' the figure by taking a hammer to its face.

It is difficult to know how glass-painters across Europe reacted to the destruction, or what they felt when they were ordered to remove and replace the work of their predecessors, or indeed works of their own. The historian Guy-Michel Leproux, who has examined the wills of the sixteenth-century glass-painters in Paris, perhaps not surprisingly comes to the conclusion that they probably remained good catholics. Perhaps in Protestant countries, as the tide turned, there were glass-painters who worried about the idolatrous nature of their work. Iconoclasm must have had a profound psychological effect on craftsmen, but the change in religion also had a devastating economic effect on the craft as commissions for church windows dried up, effectively bringing to an end centuries of tradition.

The Freemens Registers of York, a city whose connections with stained glass went back to the twelfth century and beyond bring the effects of the Reformation home, for during the whole of the second half of the sixteenth century only one glass-painter is listed, and he, Bernard Dinninckhoff, was probably a protestant refugee from Bohemia. Architecturally, it was the Elizabethan country house which took the place of the monastery and the church so that it is not surprising that amongst the finest stained glass of the Queen's reign is the armorial glazing that Dinninckhoff painted mainly in enamels in 1585 and following years for the Fairfax family of Gilling Castle, Yorkshire. Both the ideological viewpoint behind the glass and the techniques used differ from those held and employed by medieval artists; the break with the past it embodies could not be more definite.

This break in tradition was to have a profound effect on the future preservation of medieval windows. Further outbreaks of iconoclasm took place in the seventeenth century when major works by medieval glass-painters were destroyed, but almost as much damage was done by generations of glaziers who lacked the raw materials and the technical skills to maintain or restore the old glass properly. Although interest in medieval glass began to revive in the middle of the eighteenth century as part of a wider fashion for things Gothic, it was not until the Gothic Revival of the nineteenth century that antiquaries, scientists and glass-painters brought about a thorough revival of medieval techniques, iconography and styles. This recovery of the medieval pot-metal techniques was to prove a lasting contribution to the future of stained glass.

In the present climate the medium is enjoying another revival, particularly as far as domestic glass is concerned. In an age given to looking back at the past with nostalgia, the tendency is to appreciate our heritage of stained glass and view its past destruction with considerable regret. The present conservationist approach to the work of the medieval glass-painters has come to dominate stained glass studies in recent years.

In an age of increasing pollution and vandalism, it would be foolish to be too confident about the future, but at least under the auspices of the international *Corpus Vitrearum Medii Aevi* or CVMA (Catalogue of Medieval Stained Glass), founded as a result of losses during the last world war, art historians are recording and publishing all surviving medieval panels, not only in Europe, but further afield in countries like Canada and the United States, where medieval glass figures prominently in both private and museum collections. Scientific work sponsored by the Technical Committee of the CVMA is researching into problems of corrosion and examining methods of protecting medieval windows for posterity. The survival of the works of the medieval glass-painters will depend on the skill and the craftsmanship of today's conservators.

84 Arms of Sir Thomas Fairfax at Gilling Castle, Yorkshire, painted by Bernard Dinninckhoff in 1585, a spectacular example of multicoloured enamel glass-painting.

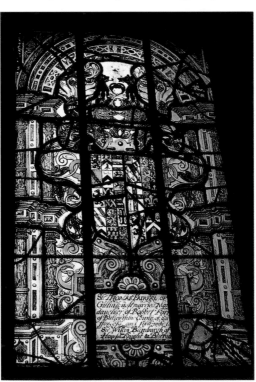

GLOSSARY

Abrasion A scraping or grinding away of a *flashed* surface to expose the white glass beneath.

Annealing A costly and rare technique described by Theophilus in which small jewels of coloured glass were added to white glass without using leads by painting around them and firing them into place.

Armature Wrought-iron framework used to support panels of stained glass and establish the formal layout of Romanesque and Early Gothic windows.

Back painting Painting applied to the exterior surface of the glass.

Cartoon A full-scale design for stained glass on parchment or paper.

Cutline A full-scale outline drawing of the leading, used for the cutting and leading of stained glass.

Enamels Enamel colours consisting of metallic oxide colouring agents and a flux of molten glass were fired onto white glass allowing multicoloured painterly effects to be achieved. They were used extensively in the sixteenth, seventeenth and eighteenth centuries.

Ferramenta The ironwork used to support panels of stained glass in the architectural framework.

Flashed glass A basic white glass to which a thin layer of colour was added when the glass was blown. Flashed ruby is the most common colour.

Grisaille Panels or windows of predominantly white glass, leaded or painted to form geometric or foliage designs.

Grozing Method of trimming or shaping pieces of glass with a grozing iron, a tool with a hook at each end which leaves a characteristic 'nibbled' edge.

Mullion An upright shaft of stone dividing a window into lights.

Pot-metal Window glass coloured throughout by the addition of metallic oxides to the molten glass during manufacture.

Quarry A diamond- or square-shaped piece of glass.

Ruby Term commonly used for red glass.

Smear shading Method of shading glass with thin washes of paint.

Stick work The removal of paint from the glass with a stick or needle before firing.

Stipple shading Method of shading glass by dabbing paint with the end of a brush.

Tracery lights Small openings in the upper part of a window.

Transom A horizontal bar of stone running across the window.

Vidimus Small-scale preparatory sketch for a stained glass window.

Yellow stain A technique developed in the early fourteenth century which colours white glass yellow, or blue glass green, by applying a solution of a silver compound to the exterior surface and firing it. Sometimes called silver stain.

FURTHER READING

Despite the extensive literature on medieval stained glass windows, surprisingly little has been written about the glaziers and glass-painters who made them and no other general book has been written on this subject. Readers seeking further information could begin by consulting two bibliographical works:

D. EVANS,
A Bibliography of Stained Glass, Cambridge, 1982.
M. H. CAVINESS and
E. R. STAUDINGER,
Stained Glass before 1540, an Annotated Bibliography, Boston, 1983.

The best introduction to the whole subject of stained glass remains:

JEAN LAFOND,
Le Vitrail, Paris, 1966, and subsequent editions.

The detailed catalogues of medieval stained glass published by the international *Corpus Vitrearum Medii Aevi* provide an unrivalled source of information on surviving windows, the workshops which made them and the techniques they used. A list of volumes both published and in preparation can be found in the most recent British volume:

T. FRENCH and D. O'CONNOR,
York Minster A Catalogue of Medieval Stained Glass, Fascicule 1, Oxford, 1987.

The following works contain more specific information on medieval glass-painters:

J. D. LE COUTEUR,
English Mediaeval Painted Glass, ch.III, 'The Mediaeval Glass Painters', London, 1926.
J. A. KNOWLES,
Essays in the History of the York School of Glass-Painting, London, 1936.
H. WENTZEL,
'Glasmaler und Maler im Mittelalter', in *Zeitschrift für Kunstwissenschaft* III (1949), 53–62.
J. LOWE,
'The Medieval English Glazier', in *Journal of the British Society of Master Glass-Painters* XIII no.2 (1961), 425–32 and XIII no.3 (1962), 492–508.
F. PERROT,
'La signature des peintres-verriers', in *Revue de l'Art* XXVI (1974), 40–5.

C. BRISAC and J-J. GRUBER,
'Le Métier de maître verrier', in *Métiers d'Art* 20 (1982).
M. P. LILLICH,
'Gothic Glaziers: Monks, Jews, Taxpayers, Bretons, Women', in *Journal of Glass Studies* 27 (1985), 72–92.
G. M. LEPROUX,
Recherches sur les Peintres-Verriers Parisiens de la Renaissance 1540–1620, Geneva, 1988.

A useful introduction to the wealth of documentation in England is:

L. F. SALZMAN,
Building in England down to 1540, ch.XI 'Glazing', London, 1952.

Further information on royal glaziers can be found in:

H. M. COLVIN, ed.,
The History of the King's Works, The Middle Ages, 1 and 2, London, 1963.

As far as technical matters are concerned R. NEWTON and S. DAVISON, *The Conservation of Glass*, London, 1988, contains an excellent introduction to glass-making and glass-painting techniques in the Middle Ages.

The most important of the medieval treatises is:

THEOPHILUS,
De Diversis Artibus/The Various Arts, ed. and trans. C. R. DODWELL, London, 1961.

An alternative edition, *On Divers Arts, the Treatise of Theophilus*, ed. J. G. HAWTHORN and C. S. SMITH, Chicago, 1963, has a less scholarly text but contains useful technical and scientific notes.

Other useful medieval treatises are:

CENNINO CENNINI,
The Craftsman's Handbook, the Italian 'Il libro dell' arte', trans. D. V. THOMPSON, New York and London, 1954, and
Il Trattato di Antonio da Pisa sulla Fabbricazione delle Vetrate Artistiche, ed. S. PEZZELLA, Perugia, 1976.

ACKNOWLEDGEMENTS

We owe a great debt to a number of stained glass artists and conservators and their staffs, who over the past few years have given us ready access to their studios. In particular, we would like to thank Keith Barley of Barley Studios, Alfred Fisher of Chapel Studios, Dennis King of G. King and Sons, Sep Waugh, glass-painter of York, and Peter Gibson of the York Glaziers Trust.

Photographic credits are given elsewhere, but we are particularly grateful to Peter Burton of the History of Art Department of the University of Manchester and the staff of the photographic section of the Royal Commission on the Historical Monuments of England and the Corpus Vitrearum Archive.

Finally, our personal thanks to Kate Harris, Roderick Brown and Stephen Croad for their generous help and encouragement.

INDEX